Ain't Gonna Study War No More

Also by Milton Meltzer

THE TERRORISTS

THE HUMAN RIGHTS BOOK

THE TRUTH ABOUT THE KU KLUX KLAN

THE BLACK AMERICANS: A HISTORY IN THEIR OWN WORDS

THE JEWISH AMERICANS: A HISTORY IN THEIR OWN WORDS

THE HISPANIC AMERICANS

THE CHINESE AMERICANS

ALL TIMES, ALL PEOPLES: A WORLD HISTORY OF SLAVERY

NEVER TO FORGET: THE JEWS OF THE HOLOCAUST

LANGSTON HUGHES: A BIOGRAPHY

A PICTORIAL HISTORY OF BLACK AMERICANS

(with Langston Hughes and C. Eric Lincoln)

MILTON MELTZER

Ain't Gonna Study War No More

The Story of America's Peace Seekers

HARPER & ROW, PUBLISHERS

To Philip McArthur

Photo credits: The Historical Society of Pennsylvania, 34;
Milton Meltzer Collection, 89; *The New Yorker*, 165; Picture
Collection, The Branch Libraries, The New York Public
Library, 18, 21, 25, 93, 129, 146, 206; Southern Christian
Leadership Conference, 224; The Bettmann Archive, 76;
War Resisters League, 269; Wide World Photos, 150, 178,
197, 238, 253, 262.

Library of Congress Cataloging in Publication Data
Meltzer, Milton, 1915–
   Ain't gonna study war no more.

   Bibliography: p.
   Summary: Presents a history of pacifism and those
who have protested against war, concentrating on war
resistance in the United States, from colonial days
up to the current movement against nuclear arms.
   1. Peace—History—Juvenile literature.   2. Pacifists
—United States—History—Juvenile literature.
3. Military service, Compulsory—United States—Draft
resisters—History—Juvenile literature.   [1. Pacifists
—History.   2. Military service, Compulsory—United
States—Draft resisters—History]   I. Title.
JX1963.M546 1985   327.1′72   84-48337
ISBN 0-06-024199-3
ISBN 0-06-024200-0 (lib. bdg.)

Designed by Barbara A. Fitzsimmons
10 9 8 7 6 5 4 3

CONTENTS

Down by the Riverside

Ain't Gonna Study
War No More

CHAPTER ONE

I Am Not Willing
to Sign My Life Over

Draft registration is preparation for war. To sign a registration card is to sign a promise—a promise to the United States government that it may take your body at any time, for any war it may see fit.

I am not willing to sign my life over to the government that brought us Vietnam, Watergate and the Trident submarine. I am not willing to withhold my protest until this country is sending troops to Latin America. . . . And I am not willing to wait until the nuclear arms race has reached its logical conclusion in a nuclear holocaust. . . .

I do not offer a legal defense. When we choose to act illegally but morally, your authority becomes irrelevant. We are acting within different frameworks of duty, and I value my own, which I like to believe affirms life, above yours, which would require

3

me to kill at the command of men I neither know nor trust.

That is why Russ Ford refused to register for the draft. He stated his reasons in 1982 in an article he wrote for a Connecticut newspaper and in a letter to the U.S. Department of Justice.

Out in Kansas, Kendal Warkentine, a member of the Mennonite church, was indicted for not registering (on grounds of religious pacifism). He wrote:

Obedience is owed to God. When we are asked to disregard what we believe to be his will we have no choice but to disobey. . . . Registration for the draft is part of the military machine in our nation. As a Christian I feel that Christ taught a way of peace. . . . I felt that to be true to this way of peace I could not register.

Kendal pleaded guilty and was sentenced by the judge. The day he was sentenced, he said:

It is to God that I owe my ultimate obedience. At the same time I believe that I should submit to the governing authorities. It is my attempt to be subject to the government while still being obedient to God that has led to my plea of guilty. . . . I know I am legally guilty of not registering, but morally I feel I am innocent. When nonregistration is based on loyalty to God I do not believe it is wrong.

4

This is a book about courage. Not the courage it takes to go into battle but the courage to organize resistance to war when a fever for it inflames the country, and the courage to refuse military service under pain of being called a coward and the threat of prison or even execution. In the 1980s, refusal to register for the draft within thirty days of a man's eighteenth birthday could bring penalties of up to five years in prison and a $10,000 fine. Yet of the 12 million or more young Americans required to register for the draft by the middle of 1984, 500,000 had not—a much higher proportion than in the early years of the Vietnam War.

At eighteen, or approaching that age, men have to decide whether or not to register for the draft. Facing that decision, a surprising number of the "me" generation is saying "not me." It appears that an antidraft, anti-intervention movement has surfaced again—a sign that a considerable number of young people may no longer blindly follow our leaders into war.

If you ask, "What war?" the box score on mass violence around the world provides the answer.

• In the past few years, 45 of the world's 164 nations have been involved in wars. Estimates of the number of people killed range from 1 million to 5 million.

• There were ten conflicts in the Middle East–Persian Gulf, another ten in Asia and Africa, seven more in Latin America, and three in Europe. Five of these were conventional wars and twenty-five were internal guerrilla struggles.

• In 1981, the forty-five nations involved in conflicts spent over $528 billion on their armed forces. The United States and the USSR and its satellites are the major suppliers of their military weapons.

Facts, facts, facts. "We are the best informed people on earth," said the poet Archibald MacLeish. "We are deluged with facts, but we have lost or are losing our human ability to *feel* them."

The young Americans who refuse publicly to register for the draft are violating the law in the hope that their willingness to accept prosecution and punishment will draw the people's attention to the facts of war. They denounce war because it destroys life, corrupts society, and violates morality. They consider U.S. military intervention in the affairs of other nations to be wrong. For the young, especially, the constant talk of nuclear war is frightening. They live with the threat of imminent annihilation. They fear that they may never reach adulthood. But is war inevitable? Are we powerless to shape our future? Cannot the superpowers—the United States and the USSR—resolve their differences peacefully?

By refusing to make that first connection with the military—registering for the draft—some young men separate themselves from the machinery of war. Their action by itself will not stop war from coming. This they know, but at least they will not take part in the killing process.

How does a soldier feel who has been through that process? Here is the voice of Alfred Döblin, a German who served in the Kaiser's army in the First World War. He speaks through Becker, a character in his novel *A People Betrayed*:

You receive a mobilization order. An agency, an office that you don't know, writes go here, go there, go to your death, to your ruin, go, so that you lose a leg, so that you get a bullet in your spine. Be careful, my boy, there will be gas, poison gas, mustard gas; swallow some. And you'll soon notice it may cost your head, your leg, your lungs, your life, and no one will ever replace them, since your mother gave all that to you just once. And you've been expecting it for a long time. During peacetime you prepared yourself for it, in the midst of your Kant and Plato. And you—don't question. You don't question, you go, you obey. The agency that issues the orders is more than God. You listen, more than to God. . . .

Then Becker asks himself:

What is it I've finally come to believe is the real evil behind it all? Not the war itself . . . the incomprehensible, incredible thing about war was—we ourselves. We, you and I, coolies, animals, without the vaguest idea, awareness or understanding . . . doing what we were told and not thinking anything about it. Yet it was our lives that were at stake, and we had been taught even as children that God himself created them and set us humans above all his other creatures. And here we were flinging them aside, our lives, as though they were dead logs, as though we had never learned anything, heard anything, and lying there numb like the subhumans who slaved to build the pyramids.

I did it and so did you, educated men who had been pumped full of Christianity, ancient and modern philosophy, Plato, Spinoza, Descartes, Kant. And in the end they had merely flowed right through us and left nothing behind, leaving us oafish slaves, brainless creatures, gasping for air, complete troglodytes, semi-apes from the stone age. How is that possible, you ask yourself, how? It was a matter of our very existence. Didn't we really believe any of it, didn't we take seriously what they told us, what we learned? Are we like barrels full of holes?

When Döblin returned from war, he had learned something. He had not been able to learn it from books. Are we different in America? Are there books we can learn from? The school histories always play up the importance of war. But they ignore, for the most part, the story of *resistance* to war. Yet resistance does have a history, and surely we should know something about it. Looking into the record, I found that no wars we fought ever had the full support of all Americans. And some of the wars—both a long time ago and very recently—were met with open and powerful resistance.

It's impossible to think of any other subject that can match this in importance—for today and for our future.

CHAPTER TWO

A Quarrelsome World

For a country with a rather short history, ours has done quite a bit of fighting. We have taken part in seven officially declared wars. And without the approval of Congress, we have sent our armed forces beyond our borders over 165 times. That comes close to one military intervention per year since the United States was founded.

If it's any comfort to know, the United States isn't more quarrelsome than the rest of the world. A scholar took the trouble to count up the wars of this planet from 1496 B.C. to A.D. 1861, a period of 3,357 years. He found there were wars during 3,310 of those years. Not a record to make anyone feel good.

But almost half of the time covered in that study was ancient history, certainly pre-Christian. Is the picture any brighter if we confine it to modern times? Another scholar tried that. He added up the wars fought between the time Columbus sailed to the New World and 1941, the year of Pearl Harbor. He reports 278 wars, in which 2,700 major battles bled countless millions.

To get back to America: While the figures make it look like we're as bloody-minded as anybody else, it's also true that many Americans have opposed military actions and have refused personally to have any part of them. They drew a line they would not cross because their consciences would not let them.

Such people are called "conscientious objectors" (COs, for short), a term that did not come into use until World War I. Before then, they were called "nonresistants." That term comes from the words of Jesus, opposing the use of violence: "Ye have heard that it hath been said, an eye for an eye and a tooth for a tooth: but I say unto you, that ye resist not evil: but whosoever shall smite thee on thy right cheek, turn to him the other also." There are several reasons—religious, moral, political—that people give for refusing to participate in war. And even the degree of refusal varies. Absolute pacifists will not cooperate with any preparation for war, let alone war itself. Others will accept some kinds of service so long as they are not forced to fight. And still others are willing to fight in "just wars," though not in wars they believe to be "unjust."

To understand these differences in point of view, perhaps it's best to see how the peace seekers developed their ideas and made them part of the history of our nation in war and peace.

We forget how many immigrants came to America to escape conscription in their homeland. They wanted to live in a country that would not force them into military service. They were among the immigrants who arrived in the earliest years of white settlement in the American colonies. Some were pacifists by conviction, opposed to war or violence of any kind. Others were weary of the wars of the Old World, when men were forced into military service, often for many long years. In the New World they hoped to live in peace.

Most of the immigrants who came to America with pacifist principles belonged in their homeland to Christian sects that opposed war on religious grounds. But we can go farther back than Christianity to find ancient religious writings against war and violence. In the China of the sixth century B.C., Lao-tzu, founder of the world religion known as Taoism, stressed love, moderation, and a nonviolent way of life. And although the Old Testament is full of battles, the ancient Jews believed that the Lord was more powerful in keeping the Israelites from harm than soldiers and weapons. To act justly would do more to prevent violent conflict than to rely on the military power of the state. In the Old Testament, some of the great Hebrew prophets anticipated the ethic of nonviolent resistance. Later, the Jewish sect of the Essenes rejected violence on principle.

In the Sermon on the Mount, Jesus develops the ethic of nonviolence and love of enemies. "Blessed are the peacemakers: for they shall be called the children of God." And he told Peter, "All they that take the sword shall perish with the sword" (Matt. 26:52). These last words are taken to mean that violence is futile in the long run. To meet violence with violence is only to perpetuate a cycle of violence that imprisons us.

Scholars believe the early Christians were probably the first individuals to renounce participation in war unconditionally. From the time of the Apostles to about A.D. 170, there is no evidence of Christians in military service. Their refusal to take part in war was one expression of their refusal to take part in the life of the world or the affairs of the state. Public life was a heathen life, and Christians withdrew from it. Military service required an oath to heathen gods, and pagan ceremonials marked many military operations. Devout Christians refused any part in idolatry.

Early Christian refusal to serve in Rome's imperial armies can be traced back to Jewish refusal to bow down before idols. The Jews were the only subject people to win from Rome exemption from military service, an exemption they desired because service entailed worship of the emperor and would offend their faith in Yahweh, the one God. (In actual fact, their exemption did not matter so much, because the emperor could get all the soldiers he needed by voluntary enlistment.) The Church began as a Jewish sect, and for a time the Romans granted Christians the privileges already allowed the Jews.

The pagan Celsus sharply criticized the Christians for enjoying the benefits of the Empire while doing nothing to ensure its preservation. He condemned them for what would today be called conscientious objection to participation in war. "If all did as the Christians," he wrote (c. 178), "there would be nothing to prevent things from getting into the hands of the barbarians"—an argument that still confronts pacifists, as we shall see later on.

Replying to Celsus, the Christian scholar Origen (A.D. 185–254) said:

Christians have been taught not to defend themselves against their enemies; and because they have kept the laws that command gentleness and love of man, they have received from God that which they would not have achieved if they were permitted to make war, though they might have been quite able to do so. . . . The more devout the individual, the more effective he is in helping the Emperor, more so than the soldiers who go into the lines and kill all the enemy troops they can. . . . The greatest warfare, in other words, is not with human enemies but with those spiritual forces which make men into enemies.

Like Origen, many early Christian writers condemned war in general and branded killing in war as murder. War was an evil, a madness, and as for the soldier, "How can he be just, who injures, hates, despoils, kills?" Peace was more to these writers than the mere absence of war: "Nothing is better than peace, by which all war is abolished." The followers of Christ must give up the old law of retaliation to walk in the ways of peace. "We who were filled with war and mutual slaughter and every wickedness," wrote Justin Martyr, "have each of us in all the world changed our weapons of war . . . swords into plows and spears into pruning hooks."

Many soldiers left the Roman army after being converted to Christianity. They felt that their new-found religion would not permit them to shed blood.

The first recorded conscientious objector was Saint Maximilianus from Numidia in North Africa. At the age of twenty-one, in the year 295, he was called up for military duty because, as the son of a Roman soldier, he, too, was bound to serve.

When he was brought before the Roman proconsul, Dion, he said he would not serve. "I will not be a soldier of this world, for I am a soldier of Christ."

"But there are Christians serving in the army," Dion replied.

"That is their business," said Maximilianus. "I cannot fight. I cannot do evil. I am a Christian."

Led away for execution as required by law, the young man proclaimed, "God lives!"

Not long after, the soldier Martin of Tours asked his commanding officer to discharge him. It was the eve of battle. "I am a soldier of Christ," Martin said. "To fight is not permissible to me." When he was accused of cowardice, Martin offered to face the enemy alone and unarmed. Do it, the officer replied. But, inexplicably, the enemy asked for peace. Martin was given his discharge, and in time he became a bishop, and a saint.

Still, soldiering was silently tolerated by the Church, and other Christians did serve in the army, both soldier converts and Christian recruits. But the official Church teaching was clearly antimilitarist. Christian teachers of this time declared that God prohibits killing, and no exception at all ought to be made to the commandment that it is always wrong to kill. The sanctity of human life is unconditional.

Under the Emperor Constantine, Christianity became the official religion of Rome (313), and the relationship between the Church and the secular power changed radically. The state accepted the Church and the Church accepted the state. Now Christians placed themselves at the service of the emperor. Going into battle in Constantine's army, they inscribed the sign of the cross on their shields and banners. Official Christianity sanctioned military service, and those who disagreed and remained nonviolent were eventually silenced. Pacifism went underground in the Church in the fourth century.

It was late in the fourth century that the classic Christian idea of the "just war" was developed. It began with Saint Augustine (354–430). He held the traditional view that the individual Christian was barred from violence on his own behalf. But, he argued, defense of one's own community was a different matter. Even in this case the command to love one's enemies even in battle was a solemn obligation of Christian faith. An attempt was made to set up

Holzschnitt aus Nr. 452. S. Augustinus, Canones. Strassburg 1490.

The idea of the "just war" began with St. Augustine, portrayed here in a 1490 print. Late in the fourth century he argued that the good Christian, barred from doing violence on his own behalf, could take arms in a war that was just.

standards for deciding which wars were right and which wrong. Over the centuries, the theory was developed and refined.

As many theologians now hold, the standards for a just war are seven:

1. War must be the last resort and used only after all other means have failed.

2. War must be declared to redress rights actually violated or for defense against unjust demands backed by the threat of force. It must not be fought simply to satisfy national pride or to further economic or territorial gain.

3. The war must be openly and legally declared by a legal government.

4. There must be a reasonable chance of winning.

5. The means used must be in proportion to the ends sought.

6. Soldiers must distinguish between armies and civilians and not kill civilians on purpose.

7. The winner must not require the utter humiliation of the loser.

It can be debated whether any war has ever satisfied all these reasonable conditions.

Although the just war theory meant the acceptance of military service under certain conditions, Christianity and violence have not been happily joined. There has rarely been a period in Christian history without its nonviolent witness. There were always Christians who rejected violence. And not only for themselves; they required their followers to do the same. They believed Christ's way was the pursuit of peace. Saint Francis of Assisi (1182–1226) is only the most notable example. He founded religious orders—for men, for women, and for lay people. The rule he voiced was: "They are not to take up deadly weapons or bear them against anyone."

In the Middle Ages, when the Holy Roman Empire dominated Europe, religion and politics were inseparable. The emperor was a Christian emperor and the pope an imperial bishop. Two powers equally ordained of God, as they believed, controlling the Christian world. Together they fought wars against enemies without, and persecuted enemies within. Opposition or criticism seemed impossible, and if it showed itself, was quickly driven underground.

During the Crusades, fought to recover the Holy Land from Islam (eleventh to fourteenth centuries), the Church plunged into extreme violence and cruelty. How hard it must have been for the voice of Christian pacifism to be heard! But there were some who all through these centuries had the courage to criticize the theory and practice of their time. They were like the early Christians in denouncing war. Only now they were not rebelling against a heathen

St. Francis of Assisi was a leading voice in rejecting the use of violence against anyone.

empire but against the worldly Church. In their opposition they formed sects, separate from the official Church. Their pacifist convictions found their source in a return to the Bible. That, in an age when it was forbidden and dangerous to possess a Bible, when only the priests could teach and interpret it. These awakened Christians went back to the fundamental ideas of Christianity, to the New Testament, and took the Sermon on the Mount as their ideal.

The Waldenses, the Lollards, and the Moravians were the main heretical groups who repudiated war in the Middle Ages. "The force of arms is altogether inadmissible in matters of religion," wrote one of their leaders. "War under any circumstances is an accursed practice."

From these peace seekers of the Middle Ages we move to the dissenters of the Protestant Reformation. Martin Luther founded the new faith in the early 1500s. Great changes took place in religious, economic, political, and cultural life. The reformers believed that the state was an institution ordained by God as necessary to man's well-being on earth. But some among them denied that government had any right to exercise control in religious matters. Rather than act against their consciences, Christians must refuse obedience and suffer the consequences. Nor could true Christians accept public office, for it would require them to do things contrary to the teachings and example of Christ. The essence of the state, they believed, was to wage war, to exact harsh punishment, and to impose oaths. Since all of these were expressly forbidden by Christ, how could a Christian participate in the state? Be a magistrate? A policeman? A soldier?

Such nonconformists called themselves "defenseless Christians" who lived by a philosophy of nonresistance. They formed the radical wing of the Protestant Reformation. In England the nonconformists created the Quaker Society of Friends; in Germany, the Dunkards (or Dunkers) and the Moravian Church. And religious sects of this kind spread across Europe to advance the new truth they found in Jesus Christ. Determined to follow his original way, the sects committed themselves to the pursuit of peace.

They carried this dedication with them when they migrated to the New World. Shortly before the American Revolution there were 60,000 of them rooted in the colonies, living by their dissenting peace tradition. Up to the twentieth century their vision would be the foundation of organized peace action in America.

CHAPTER THREE

These Fanatical Quakers

The Quakers were among the first dissenters to bring pacifism to America. Quakerism grew out of the same thinking as the other radical sects of their time. The Quaker leader was George Fox (1624–1691), son of an English weaver and himself a cobbler wandering in search of spiritual truth. He felt something was terribly wrong with the brutal life of an England torn by civil war. How could men learn to live by the ideal described in the Bible? After losing hope in all political and religious authority, he found his truth in a faith that the Divine Spirit could speak directly to man. There could be a continuing revelation if man opened his heart to Christ. Neither university degrees nor study of the scriptures nor the preaching of a learned man was necessary. You must only recognize the Christ within yourself, he said.

Fox and his followers called themselves Friends in the Truth or simply Friends. Their enemies also had a name—Quakers—for these seekers who trembled with the inner spirit. The Society of Friends was established in 1652 and went out to take the

George Fox, an English cobbler, formed the Society of Friends, called Quakers. They stood firmly against all wars, whether religious or worldly, and often suffered for their beliefs.

truth to all corners of Britain. Everywhere they went they met persecution, were accused of being in league with the devil or plotting to overthrow the government. They were opposed to formal religion, they refused to swear oaths, they would not doff their hats to authority. Fox was offered a captaincy in Oliver Cromwell's army but refused it, saying he "lived in the virtue of that life and power that took away the occasion of all wars."

Not all the early Quakers were pacifists, for some did serve with Cromwell. But by 1660 the Quakers as a group took a firm stand against war. In a declaration of beliefs they said:

We utterly deny all outward wars and strife and fightings with outward weapons, for any end or under any pretence whatever, and we do certainly know, and so testify to the world, that the spirit of Christ, which leads us into all truth, will never move us to fight and war against any man with outward weapons, neither for the kingdom of Christ, nor for the kingdom of this world.

Labeled a "fanatical" sect, the Quakers were often imprisoned in the first decades of their growth. Eight times was Fox himself put into "nasty, stinking" jails where he and others suffered beating and branding, and hundreds died of hunger and pain. Willing to sacrifice for their beliefs, some fifteen thousand Quakers served prison terms up to 1689, when the Act of Toleration was passed. It provided a measure of legal recognition to the rights of conscience.

Persecution did not shatter the movement, though some Friends fell away. The Friends grew rapidly, drawing in people of all social classes and levels of learning. Fox's message of direct dealings between God and man attracted such distinguished people as William Penn, son of a nobleman, who established Pennsylvania as a home in America for the new sect. Women took a prominent part early in the movement. If God was in everyone, then women as well as men could be chosen by the Inner Light to be ministers.

The strength of the Friends lay in their simple organization. They established a structure of monthly, quarterly, and yearly meetings. In them each member is free to act upon his insights. The group is there to check and counterbalance excesses, at the same time that it nourishes the freedom of the individual. Under persecution, the Quakers forged an intense loyalty to their group and a tender concern for one another that strengthened their resistance to hardship.

The Quakers lived their pacifism for the sake of personal, inner peace. Publicly they proclaimed it as the path to Christ's early kingdom. For them, pacifism was not a retreat from the world. Wherever they lived they opposed, for reasons of conscience, militia drills, oath taking, jury service, and religious taxes.

They settled in most of the Atlantic coast colonies, from New England down into Georgia. At the end of the colonial period there were some 50,000 Quakers in a total American population of about 2.5 million. In each of their communities they tried to create a fellowship dedicated to building a life without violence. The great majority of them were ordinary people, farmers and artisans mostly, different from the rich and cultivated upper crust of colonial society. As they strove to live in peace, they demonstrated how practice could be in tune with principle.

In New England, a small number of Quakers tried to make their homes in the settlements established earlier by the Puritans. They swiftly discovered that this new America was no peaceful paradise.

From the first, the reality was conflict between whites and Native Americans as the settlers struggled for survival. The Puritan colonists believed the Indians were hardly human, and therefore the land they lived upon was open territory to be grabbed at will. William Bradford, a leader of the Puritans who founded Plymouth Colony, saw America as "vast and unpeopled—fruitful and fit for habitation, being devoid of all civil inhabitants, where there are only savages and brutish men, which range up and down, little otherwise than wild beasts. . . ."

The Puritans' ignorance and distrust of their neighbors led them to attack the Indians again and again. The Puritans saw themselves as Christian soldiers crusading in defense of the True Faith. For the Indians, the outcome was elimination of their power to resist and loss of their land. For the Puritans, victory meant regeneration of their souls, their church, and their fortunes.

The small minority of Quakers living within the Puritan communities would not take up arms against the Indians. During King Philip's War (1675–76), several Quakers refused the command to go out and fight. For their disobedience they were forced to run the gauntlet. The harsh and unfair policy of the Puritans clashed with the Quaker way of dealing with the Indians. The Indians retaliated for Puritan atrocities by raiding outlying settlements and killing whites. The Puritans' violence thereby placed the unarmed Quakers in as much danger as the Puritans. But despite that, most Quakers remained loyal to their peace convictions and would not take up arms even in self-defense. The Indians recognized their peaceable ways and usually left them alone.

In Puritan Massachusetts and most of the other colonies, the Quakers were seen as a troublesome sect and persecuted for their unacceptable beliefs. As soon as the first Quakers arrived in Massachusetts in the 1650s, the alarmed Puritans took severe measures to drive them out. They banished some; on others they imposed heavy fines, whippings, ear croppings, tongue borings, and even execution.

Throughout the colonies the Quakers upset the established order by refusing to serve in any colonial militia. The militia system had been brought to the colonies by the earliest English settlers. All able-bodied men between roughly the ages of sixteen and sixty were required by law to give military service. Under penalty of fines for delinquency, each man had to maintain his own uniform, rifle or musket, and ammunition and to report on muster days for inspection and drill. Militiamen were part-time soldiers who were not called into active service except to defend their homes in the event of foreign invasion, Indian uprising, or a similar emergency.

Refusal by a Quaker to serve in the colonial militia brought about the first recorded case of an American persecuted for conscientious objection. In 1658 Richard Keene, a Maryland Quaker, refused to be trained as a soldier. Fining him heavily, the angry sheriff drew his cutlass and struck young Keene on

This 1656 print depicts Quakers in Massachusetts being persecuted for their beliefs. A Quaker who refused to serve in the colonial militia was the first American to be punished for conscientious objection.

the shoulder, saying, "You dog, I could find in my heart to split your brains."

An early trial of Quaker peace beliefs in Massachusetts came during war with the Indians. The colony passed a law that imprisoned anyone who refused to bear arms or was unwilling to pay a fine in place of service. The Quaker John Smith, aged twenty-two, was called to join the militia in 1703. He refused, was tried, and was fined. When he would not pay the fine, he was sentenced to hard labor in the fort at Boston for as long as would pay the fine and costs. The judge said only "ignorance and a perverse nature" could lead anyone to refuse to fight the enemy. Smith replied that "it was not obstinacy, but duty to God, according to conscience, and religious persuasion," which prevailed with him "to refuse to bear arms, or learn war."

Sent to the fort, Smith refused to perform military labor. After four months, the governor released him. He then joined the crew of a Quaker merchant's ship bound for England. When it docked at Plymouth, he was seized by the British for service in the royal navy. At sea, a French ship gave them battle, and Smith was placed at a gun and ordered to fire. He refused and was hauled on deck and ordered to work. Again he refused because on a naval vessel this would be war work. An enraged officer had him whipped savagely. For thirteen months at sea his life was made hell, until the ship returned to Plymouth and the captain said he never wanted to see this reluctant sailor again.

Many young Quakers were put in jail for conscientious objection during the colonial wars. Quakers refused to work on fortifications, would not supply provisions for those who did work, and for nonpayment of fines were jailed again and again. Those Quakers who did accept military duty were dealt with by their societies and disowned, unless they showed proper contrition.

In Virginia in the 1750s, when men were drafted for the militia, seven young Quakers resisted and were arrested. In court they said they would comply with the law in all other things, but "to bear arms or fight we could not." The judge then ordered them to work at the forts. This, too, they would not do; they were sent under military escort to a frontier post commanded by a young Colonel George Washington. On the hard four-day hike the seven would not eat the king's food and went hungry. Nor would they even answer roll call three times daily, as this would be admission of their status as soldiers. A furious captain ordered one of the Quakers to be whipped as an example, but when a soldier protested that it was wrong to punish a man for his religious scruples, the captain withdrew his order.

Arrived at the fort, the men were thrown into the guardhouse for five weeks, until Colonel Washington returned from a tour of the frontier. At first he threatened to give them five hundred strokes each unless they would work on the fort, but, impressed perhaps by the Quakers' adherence to their principles, he relented. They were kept under house arrest in the town to the end of the year, when their legal term of service was ended.

The best-known peace advocate in early American history is, of course, William Penn (1644–1718). A

Young William Penn, the highborn Englishman who became a Quaker. He founded the colony of Pennsylvania in the hope of building a model community that would live in peace created out of justice.

high-born Englishman who became a Quaker, he accepted proprietorship of a huge tract of land in settlement of a family debt with King Charles II, and called it Pennsylvania. To Penn, this was not just a business venture. He wanted Pennsylvania to be the one place where persecuted Quakers could escape England and build a model Christian community that would live in planned social harmony. He dreamed of a society flourishing in peace growing out of justice. The constitution he drew up provided for popular representative government and complete religious freedom. The Friends' message was for all people, whatever their rank, nation, or race. It was a vision that raised human personality to a new dignity. The expression of Penn's faith is found in his 1682 treaty with the Indians. He told them:

The great Spirit who made me and you knows that I and my friends have a hearty desire to live in peace and friendship with you, and to serve you to the utmost of our power. It is not our custom to use hostile weapons against our fellow creatures, for which reason we have come unarmed. . . . I will consider you as the same flesh and blood with the Christians, and the same as if one man's body were to be divided into two parts. . . .

Penn stood for peaceable negotiation of differences. By patience and not by the gun, Quakers kept conflict to a minimum and made violence a rarity. They insisted that Indian land be purchased at a fair price and not be stolen, that Indians have trial by jury composed of Indians and whites, and that grievances be arbitrated at the time of dispute. Nor would they follow the common custom of enslaving Indians. The Indians came to trust the Quakers, and in turn the Quakers trusted the Indians.

During the wars that bloodied the frontier, the Quakers objected to giving money and raising troops. Adopt a just policy toward the Indians, they argued, and there will be no war. Their wisdom was proved by the fact that for over seventy years peace prevailed between the settlers of Pennsylvania and their Indian neighbors. There were, as well, almost no border raids or Indian uprisings in the other colonies where Quakers held political power—Rhode Island, New Jersey, and North Carolina. Even in the non-Quaker colonies where white settlers cheated and drove out Indians, the Quaker settlements were left in peace by the Indians.

The peace, which lasted seventy years, was finally broken. Anti-Quaker forces during the French and Indian War of the 1750s pressured the Quaker legislators so hard for military action that the Quakers withdrew from the government of Pennsylvania. The Quakers had been forced into such compromise in the conduct of public affairs that they felt the spiritual life of their society was endangered. So they turned their backs on the exercise of power rather than accept measures they could not in good conscience support.

While as a group the Friends always rejected war in principle, individual members were often divided on the precise way to act in specific circumstances. Those with the most sensitive conscience took what others considered extreme positions for peace. The taxes levied for the wars of the 1750s were paid by many Quakers. But John Woolman (1720–1772) was one of the Friends who would not do that. "To refuse the active payment of a Tax which our Society generally paid was exceedingly disagreeable," he said, "but to do a thing contrary to my Conscience appeared yet more dreadful." If Quakers would not fight, how could they allow their money to do so? A few Dunkards and Mennonites joined in opposition to the French and Indian War by refusing to pay taxes.

Woolman, a tailor from New Jersey, was the oldest son in a family of thirteen children. He was a quiet, serious boy who enjoyed books. In his teens he did his best "to excel in the art of foolish jesting and to promote mirth." But by the age of twenty he had turned to a godly life and become one of the shining lights of the Quaker faith. An early abolitionist, he wrote a pioneering tract against slavery, and persuaded Quaker slaveholders, against their self-interest, to free their human property. He pointed out the hypocrisy of calling war wrong while holding in bondage by force one's fellow beings. His was a great influence in launching the Friends on their antislavery career.

Woolman supported the young conscientious objectors to war of his day. In time he came to believe that the cause of war, slavery, and all social evil was to be found in greed and ownership of too much property. His life and work exemplify the Quaker idea of "true concern." It means to feel so keenly the plight of others that one's duty is to take action. The journal he kept is moving testimony to how one person can alter human relations by being simple, decent, and loving. Always gentle, Woolman was unyielding in his quest for peace and justice.

A nonviolent world was Woolman's hope. He saw peace as a total way of life, not just a special interest of the Quakers. The degree to which he would go in this is set down in his journal:

It requires great self-denial and resignation of ourselves to God to attain that state wherein we can freely cease from fighting when wrongfully invaded, if by our fighting there was a probability of overcoming the invaders. Whoever rightly attains to it, does in some degree feel that spirit in which our Redeemer gave his life for us.

Here, back in the eighteenth century, Woolman gave his answer to a question that is always raised for COs: Would you fight if your country is attacked? When people ask that question, they are really suggesting that willingness to fight is the test of someone's patriotism. COs love their country as much as anybody else. By saying no to the war system, Woolman was speaking out of his deep conviction that killing is wrong no matter what the circumstances. Later we will see how COs meet this question in the various kinds of war America fights.

CHAPTER FOUR

Nonresisters
in a Revolutionary Time

The Quakers were only one of the religious groups opposed to war. Several other peace sects were among the early immigrants to America. Like the Quakers, they held that the state has no authority over matters of conscience. That belief brought them persecution in Europe and again in colonial America.

Many of these peace churches—the Mennonites, the Brethren, the Amish—take literally the New Testament injunction to "resist not evil," and their members are called "nonresistants." Most of them separate themselves from the world, especially its political aspects. Governments rely on force or violence to maintain their authority and power. So these religious sects forbid participation in government.

They will not hold office or vote, for such action would involve inflicting violence or electing those who would.

In practice, these sects obey the civil authority, but only up to the point of not themselves using violence. They pay taxes even when the money is used to support war. If drafted, they have in the past paid to be exempted or accepted alternative service. This, they believe, is consistent with not resisting evil. And while they accept the authority of the state—and its use of punishment—as necessary to control human corruption and crime, they refuse to take part in the state's affairs because that would bring sin upon themselves.

Knowing they cannot ignore government's power nor overcome it, these groups withdraw into their own rural communities, where they live "a Bible-centered, church-centered, vocational nonresistance." Pacifism is part of their rejection of worldly power, and a sign of their readiness to suffer in the world for Christ's sake. "Our weapons are not swords and spears," said Menno Simons (1496–1561), founder of the Mennonite sect, "but patience, silence, and hope, and the word of God." His followers would suffer for Christ, but not kill for Him.

But withdrawal is not the way of the Quakers. They do not see their church as an island where they can shelter from a sinful world. Theirs is an activist vision, requiring them to help create a world of peace and justice.

That openness led William Penn to welcome other radical sects to Pennsylvania. The first group of German Mennonites migrated to Germantown near Philadelphia in 1683. And soon after came the Church of the Brethren (or Dunkards), the Schwenkfelders, and the Moravians. A smaller pacifist sect, the Rogerenes, settled in New England.

In colonial times all the peace churches resisted military duty in one way or another. Once the Moravians moved their entire community to avoid war, leaving Georgia in 1739 rather than fight the Spaniards along the Florida border. During the French and Indian War, the Brethren refused to serve personally. But they met the demands the military made upon their property. They let their horses and wagons be requisitioned, so long as their young men were not made to shed blood in defense of the state.

From the earliest days, the colonies adopted measures to assure there would be soldiers enough to meet military needs. The first settlement at Jamestown in Virginia was the first to introduce conscription for the militia system, and in 1663 Plymouth Colony required all able-bodied men to undergo military training. Conscription was common in the colonies, except for Pennsylvania, but always on the local level. By the American Revolution, there were over 650 ordinances to raise and maintain militias. The thirteen colonies never tried to centralize a draft system, nor did that happen within each colony.

Varied as the local draft laws were, two facts about their effects are plain: (1) the rich got off easy—they could avoid the draft by paying cash, supplying munitions, or providing for a paid substitute; (2) the poor were stuck—they could not afford the options of the rich, and they were often so badly off they took cash to serve in place of the rich. The contrast between treatment of rich and poor was so harsh, it moved Benjamin Franklin to ask "whether it be just in a community, that the richer part should compel the poor to fight for them and their properties for such wages as they think fit to allow, and punish them if they refuse?"

As time passed, the persecution of radical peace sects let up to a degree. The colonies worked out some measure of accommodation with the demand for liberty of conscience, and on the basic issue of military service, the peace groups won recognition, at least here and there. Refusal to serve on grounds of conscience was respected in Massachusetts from 1661, Rhode Island from 1673, Pennsylvania from 1757. (The acceptance of conscientious objection to military service goes back to the Netherlands in 1575, when William of Orange granted it to Dutch Mennonites.)

But those who would not serve were required to do other things. Exemption for conscientious objectors was not complete (except in Rhode Island, where the Quakers were dominant). It was hedged in by terms that Quakers in particular could not accept. They would not pay the required fine in place of service (they believed that to be wrong in principle), nor would they hire a substitute. Such stubbornness often brought punishment through seizure of their property, or jailing.

With the coming of the American Revolution, Quakers and other pacifist groups found themselves in great trouble. To make a revolution was to make war, and that they refused to do. The patriots denounced them bitterly as traitors. But the pacifist groups did not necessarily support the pro-British Loyalists, either. The Pennsylvania Quakers spoke out boldly in criticism of both sides:

We did not approve the proceedings of the British Ministry, which irritated the Americans; we thought them ill-advised and . . . wicked; we would have joined with our fellow-citizens in peaceful legal resistance to them and have suffered . . . for the principles of liberty and justice. But we do not believe in

44

revolutions, and we do not believe in war. . . . We are out of the whole business and will give aid and comfort to neither party.

Yet when the radical patriots decided for revolution, peace was declared as one of their purposes. Had not British rule over the colonies brought constant conflict? Would it not be better to get rid of monarchy with its wars and conquests and replace it with the peaceful life of a model republic? So Tom Paine argued in 1776. With Britain as "our master," he wrote,

we became enemies to the greatest part of Europe, and they to us; and the consequence was war inevitable. By being our own masters, independent of any foreign one, we have Europe for our friends, and the prospect of an endless peace among ourselves.

And Thomas Jefferson, in the Declaration of Independence, voiced a long-standing belief when he asserted that the stationing of thousands of troops in the colonies and the king's attempt to make them independent of civil authority were among the reasons for revolution. That antimilitarist spirit bred into colonial bones was what made it so hard for the new nation to raise the Continental Army. The colonists remembered the endless wars in Europe. They feared a large standing army and did not like

45

giving up local militia they could control to a national fighting force. The Continental Congress was miserly in funding the army, and enlistments were erratic and brief.

Like the Quakers, the other-world peace sects—the Mennonites, Dunkards, Shakers—took a neutral position during the war. But unlike the Quakers, they bought exemption from military service and willingly did war-related work. They were "accountable to none but God," they maintained:

> It is our fixed principle rather than take up Arms to defend our King, our Country, or our Selves, to suffer all that is dear to us to be rent from us, even Life itself, and this we think not out of Contempt to Authority, but that herein we act agreeable to what we think is the mind and Will of our Lord Jesus.

In the year the Revolution was launched, the Quaker Anthony Benezet (1713–1784) published one of America's first pacifist pamphlets, *Thoughts on the Nature of War*. He condemned war as "the premeditated and determined destruction of human beings, creatures fashioned after the image of God." He combed history to show that people prospered peacefully until lust for wealth and power over men provoked war that lasted until exhaustion induced peace. That pattern could be broken only if Christians lived responsibly by the law of love and got their governments to do the same. He urged the rebel leaders to forsake war as a means of achieving their ends. Benezet took his message beyond Quakers to the broad public, asking audiences not simply to pray for peace but to *act* against war, and to refuse to pay war taxes.

The Quakers and the other peace sects petitioned in support of their principled objection to war. But the new nation had no settled policy toward conscientious objectors. Instead there was a mosaic of local or state law, confused and contradictory. Some laws simply ignored the whole issue, others provided for alternative service, fines, confiscation of property, or conditional exemption of varying degree.

There was never an attempt to develop a national position. It might have come out of General Washington's several appeals for a centralized draft, but each time the Congress only rebuked him. At one point, reacting to protests against the leniency shown locally to some COs, the Congress advised COs to "contribute liberally, in this time of universal calamity, to the relief of their distressed Brethren in the several Colonies, and to do all other service to their oppressed country, which they can consistently with their Religious Principles." This did support conscientious objection in a limited way.

In the long run, each colony devised some sort of draft that would deliver its quota for the Continental Army. But local defense needs always got first call. Both the colonies and the Congress relied heavily on cash bounties to induce volunteers to sign up. Sums ranged from the low of $200 offered by the Continentals to the $1,000 by New Jersey.

Resistance to military duty ran alongside the effort to raise a revolutionary army. A great many people— as is usually the case!—wanted no part of this war or any war. Unlike members of the peace sects, they had no principled position. They simply wanted to be let alone, to live their normal, everyday lives. And when the call to military service came, they sought any way out.

In two counties of Virginia, such men destroyed draft records, and in a third, men of draft age staged a sit-in protest. Resistance was also felt within the services. About 50 percent of the militia deserted during the war. The losses were so bad that states offered huge fees for turning in deserters, and informers were promised draft exemption. To avoid fighting or to remain loyal to the crown, some sixty thousand people fled to exile in Canada.

The king's army too was plagued by desertion. British soldiers shipped to fight in America were poor men "pressed" into service by false promises or kidnaped to fill a quota. Their treatment was cruel and they deserted in large numbers.

So there was much opposition to the Revolutionary War; but only a part of it was based upon pacifist principles. Outside the peace sects, clergy aided the war as chaplains, recruiting agents, and propagandists. Some even fought as soldiers. To these clergymen, armed opposition to what was seen as British tyranny was justified. Not to the Quakers. They rejected the method of war and would not support a cause that was being pressed by force of arms. So long as the Americans used peaceful methods to oppose the crown's policies, they had the support of many Quakers. The Quakers drew back when emotions flared and violence erupted, suspecting armed rebellion was next.

After the Declaration of Independence, the Society of Friends asked members to withdraw from political life, to refrain from paying taxes or fees in place of military service, and to take no part in any business connected with the war. Town and country Quakers argued with neighbors and strangers—whether patriot or Tory—seeking to convert them to the pacifist view, and some succeeded in getting others to bear testimony against war. Quakers witnessed for peace too by doing relief work for the civilian sufferers of war, "without distinction of sects or parties." This would become typical of Quaker humanitarian aid in many wars to come.

The Quaker objector had to face paying a fine or hiring a substitute to replace him in military duty. These costs varied in amount from colony to colony and often from year to year. Failure to pay brought seizure of goods or imprisonment for those who had no property. If the Friends had been willing to pay fines, most of their COs would have suffered little. But the society refused compromise on this issue and Quakers suffered heavy losses. Houses, barns, furniture, horses, cattle, tools, were taken from them, often far beyond the value of the fine they refused to pay.

Those who broke Quaker discipline were disowned, unless they showed due contrition. Only a small percentage violated their witness; perhaps five hundred members paid fines and another thousand accepted military service, the great majority of them joining the revolutionary army. It was a painful thing, to oust the nonpacifists, but the Society felt strengthened by the test.

Soon another danger confronted the Quakers. By 1777 most state legislatures were demanding a loyalty oath. Citizens had to renounce allegiance to the king and swear loyalty to the Continental cause.

Quakers opposed all oath taking because it invaded the religious right of people to think what they pleased in the privacy of their hearts. And taking the oath in this instance would be giving consent to the decision of war. In Pennsylvania, where all schoolmasters were required to take the oath, many Quakers gave up their livelihoods rather than compromise.

The payment of taxes during the war was an issue intensely debated by the Quakers. Taxes were of three kinds: war taxes for a specific military purpose; general or mixed taxes, where only a part (but which part?) went to finance the war; and routine taxes for upkeep of highways, support of the poor, and so on. It was easy to see why the first tax should be opposed. On the second—mixed taxes—there was a split, with some refusing to pay and some not. On the last kind, no general rule was adopted, although some Quakers would not pay taxes of any kind in this war because it acknowledged a government set up by violent revolution.

Others pledged to continue tax resistance *after* the war, in order to oppose preparation for a possible next war. After the Revolution, many Quakers continued to refuse because taxes were being used to pay war debt, and therefore were essentially war taxes. That problem of what to do about taxes has troubled war resisters down to today.

During a war that lasted seven years and consumed the country, there were many other activities that inevitably touched the military in some way. And these, too, concerned the Quakers. They would do no work for the military, make no war materials, provide no supplies. Any business or trade even remotely linked to the war effort would compromise the purity of their witness for peace. And to make personal profit out of such actions worsened the offense. Friends in some places were not even allowed to attend military displays or witness troops marching. They were bound to withdraw from all aspects of private or public life touching in any way on either the British or American war effort.

When the war ended in 1783, with American independence recognized by Great Britain, the peace sects soon adapted themselves to the new republic. After George Washington was elected the country's first President, a delegation of Quakers visited him. They told the President, "We can take no part in warlike measures on any occasion or under any power but we are bound in conscience to lead quiet and peaceable lives. . . . We feel our hearts affectionately drawn toward thee." Washington thanked them and added that he knew their "principles and conduct," and that despite his disagreement with their pacifism, he believed that "the conscientious scruples of all men should be treated with great delicacy and tenderness." He hoped earnestly "that the laws may always be as extensively accommodated to them, as a due regard to the protection and essential interest of the nation may justify and permit."

Some Americans of that time had questioned whether the use of arms to win freedom from their British rulers was justified. Could independence have been gained by peaceful means? There were ardent patriots who thought so. The foremost was John Dickinson (1732–1808), a Pennsylvania Quaker. The democratic idea ingrained in the Quaker belief had made him a lover of liberty. He took the lead in shaping public sentiment, writing key state documents on the colonists' case as well as passionate appeals to the king and the English people. But he would not sign the Declaration of Independence. Not because he did not wish independence, but because he thought it too soon. He wanted to use a myriad means of nonviolent resistance that might secure honorable claims, rather than to plunge into war. If more American statesmen had thought as he did, might diplomacy have gained all that was secured at the tragic cost of war?

Half a century after independence, another Christian pacifist, the young Unitarian Sylvester Judd

(1813–1853), preached his protest against war. He shocked patriotic ears by using the American Revolution as his example of the waste of war. Like Dickinson, he approved independence, but he was convinced armed rebellion had not been necessary to gain it. Violence once begun provoked more violence until war engulfed both sides. This, even though many influential people in both Britain and America had been against an armed contest to decide the issue. Without going into the details of Judd's argument, let's just say he concluded that independence might have been won "peaceably, without spilling of a drop of blood." His case against this holiest of American wars would be echoed in the work of later historians taking a fresh look back on other American wars.

CHAPTER FIVE

A Most Unpopular War

The young republic rising out of the Revolutionary War now faced the task of self-government. The machinery at hand was the Articles of Confederation, adopted in 1781. When this system rapidly proved too weak and inadequate, it was agreed that a strong central authority was badly needed. Delegates from the thirteen states met in Philadelphia to draft a new constitution.

After it was finished, a great cry was raised when the people learned the draft constitution contained no bill of rights. They knew the lesson of governmental oppression in Britain and wanted stronger armor against tyranny. But not until the first Congress of the United States met in 1789 was the Bill of Rights, presented by James Madison, debated and approved.

In his original proposal for what became the Second Amendment, Madison included this passage: "A well regulated militia, composed of the body of the people, being the best security of a free state, the right of the people to keep and bear arms shall not be infringed, but no person religiously scrupulous shall be compelled to bear arms."

During the debate on this clause, a Mr. Gerry objected because the people in power would decide those who were religious objectors, and excuse them from bearing arms. This might destroy the militia. Mr. Jackson proposed that objectors be excused upon paying an equivalent. But Mr. Sherman pointed out that many COs would refuse to get substitutes or pay a fee. And there were some members of the peace sects who *would* defend their country, notwithstanding the religious principles of their society.

Another member contended that getting a substitute was the same thing as turning out yourself to fight. The clause did not belong in the Constitution because the matter could be left to the legislature. "It will," he said, "always possess humanity enough to indulge this class of citizens in a matter they are so desirous of."

Mr. Scott also objected to the clause. Not that

he wanted to deprive the many sects who were religiously scrupled on this point, but because he wanted to guard against those who were of no religion. Religion is on the decline, he said, and when it is generally discarded, he feared many persons would still use the pretext to get excused from bearing arms.

Mr. Boudinot urged the provision be kept in. The militia can't depend on COs anyhow, he said. What justice is there in compelling them to bear arms when they would rather die than use them? He mentioned several instances of oppression on this point that had occurred during the Revolutionary War. He wanted to show the world that the United States "takes proper care not to interfere with the religious sentiments of any person." By striking out the clause, he concluded, "we would lead people to believe the government intends to compel all citizens to bear arms."

In deciding the issue, twenty-two voted to keep the clause in, but twenty-four voted to strike it out. So it was dropped from the Second Amendment of the Bill of Rights.

Why a majority of the convention did not adopt the clause is not clear, since the majority of the states did have some such rule. Perhaps it was left to the states because no one at the time was proposing a national draft. But without such a provision in the Constitution, the Supreme Court has often observed that exemption of COs from military service is a privilege, not a right. What Congress can give, it can take away. Nevertheless, it would prove hard in the future to eliminate a privilege that had been extended so long.

After the American Revolution, the standing army dropped to eighty men. The Constitution permitted the federal government to use state militia to put down insurrection, repel invasion, and execute the laws of the Union. Unhappy with this state of affairs, Secretary of War Henry Knox called in 1790 for a federal draft and a national militia. But his proposal was knocked on the head by a Congress fearful of military rule.

A few years later Benjamin Banneker, the black astronomer, proposed that the federal government establish a peace office. His idea was developed in detail by the humanitarian Benjamin Rush, a Philadelphia physician who had been Surgeon General of the Continental Army. He urged that such a national peace office—a Secretary of Peace?—create a system of free schools to teach pacifism. As we've seen, schoolbooks usually focus on the necessity of wars, and the glory of fighting in them. The peaceful ways of settling differences are all too often ignored.

The office would work to eliminate military parades, titles, and uniforms and open antiwar museums displaying collections of swords beaten into plowshares. What Dr. Rush wanted was to nourish a culture of peace and wipe out the glamor of war. At this distance the proposal may sound odd, and nothing came of it, but it pointed to a problem bothering peace seekers ever since: how to make quiet peace as attractive as heroic war.

Meanwhile, though these were years of peace, the state militias continued their conscription. Where Quakers and the other peace sects were granted exemption, they still had to pay a small sum in exchange. This the Quakers as a body refused to do, and as before, wherever the militia officers took their jobs seriously, that refusal caused the Quakers loss of property or jailing. Quite often, however, the community did not believe that in peacetime it mattered that much, and they left the peace people alone.

And perhaps foreseeing that America might become involved in more wars in the future, Quakers argued for their absolutist position, the refusal of all conditional exemption from military service, basing their case primarily on the civil liberties of all freeborn Americans. Freedom of opinion was the birthright—the constitutional right—of every citizen, in religion as in other concerns. If a man's conscience, or his religion, forbids him to do military service, then isn't his freedom limited if he is required to pay a penalty for permission to follow his conscience? That conscience itself is an inalienable right.

More, isn't it an injustice, the Quakers argued, to confine freedom of conscience to the realm of mere thought and not to extend it also to action flowing from thought? The Friends and other peace sects, since their beginnings, had always held it to be wrong for Christians to bear arms. To oblige them to bear arms unless they paid a penalty was to force them either to refuse obedience to the law of their country or to violate what they most solemnly believed was a law of God.

Historian of pacifism Peter Brock puts it this way:

The Quaker, in following his conscience and his God in refusing to obey a man-made law and in patiently suffering the consequences, was in fact defending at the same time the civil rights and the constitutional liberties of all free Americans.

In June 1812 the United States declared war on Britain and prepared to invade Canada. Pacifist beliefs and the government attitude toward them were put to the test. This, wrote Professor Samuel Eliot Morison, proved to be "the most unpopular war that this country ever waged." The Congress was closely divided in its vote to go to war, and the armed forces could not raise half the manpower they wanted; the Congress provided for fifty thousand recruits, but less than ten thousand signed up for the one-year term of service. In Massachusetts the governor called for a public fast of atonement for America's attack upon Britain. Bankers refused to make war loans. Harvard gave five honorary degrees to outspoken antiwar critics. On Nantucket, islanders calmly declared their neutrality: they would sit out the war. And soon after the fighting began, a mob in Newburyport, Massachusetts, tried to free a group of British prisoners of war. In 1814 popular defiance was voiced at Hartford, Connecticut, where Federalists met to protest the war and demand a changed defense policy.

How did America get into that war? It had won its independence, but that did not guarantee that the young Republic would not be drawn into the wars of Europe accompanying the French Revolution and the rise of Napoleon. With the renewal of European war in 1804, English sailors had deserted by the hundreds and signed up on Yankee ships. The British navy stopped these ships and dragged off the suspected deserters, taking many Americans with them. It was "mistaken identity," the British said.

The United States complained, but the kidnaping of Americans went on for years. Meanwhile, New England merchants were making millions conducting a good part of the neutral trade with both warring countries, England and France, but especially England. There were other reasons: Along the Western frontier, beyond the Appalachians, the farmers resented English incitement to Indian warfare. With a greedy eye fixed on farmland north of the American border, they called for an invasion of British Canada; they wanted England crushed and driven from the continent. The land-hungry Western warhawks in Congress kept shouting, "National honor must be avenged!" and in the end a reluctant President Madison proclaimed the second war against Great Britain.

In New England, many ministers condemned the War of 1812 as immoral and unnecessary. War under even favorable conditions was a terrible calamity, they said, but to be just, a war had to be necessary. And had the government done all it could to obtain justice and preserve peace? New England's governors refused to call out the militias. Where was the invasion that would justify it? Merchants were trading illegally with the enemy and bankers were loaning more money to the enemy than to their own government. We should organize a peace party, urged the Massachusetts Legislature. "Let your disapproval of this war be heard loud and deep," it advised the people. Fifty-three towns sent delegates to Northampton for a convention that declared the war to be "neither just, necessary, nor expedient" and urged the President to sue for peace. Other maritime and commercial states, such as New York, New Jersey, and Delaware, also opposed the war.

The country simply was not united behind the war. So hard was it to recruit troops that in 1814 Congress considered passing a draft law. In the debate on the matter, Daniel Webster called conscription a great evil and denied that the Constitution gave the federal government the right to draft soldiers. In his passionate speech he said: "The question is nothing less than whether the most essential rights of personal liberty shall be surrendered, and despotism embraced in its worst form." If such an unconstitutional and illegal law was adopted, he advised the states to prevent its execution. "This nation," he said, is "not yet in a temper to submit to conscription."

Both the House and the Senate approved a draft bill, but before it could become law, the war ended.

Meanwhile, however, not only the Federalist Party but many prominent Republicans were lukewarm about the war. And outside New England the country was by no means united in support of it.

As the demand for men became heavier, the peace

sects were pressed harder. In Virginia, Quakers who refused to serve or pay fines were hauled off to prison. A small minority in that slaveholding state, they were given a harder time than their brethren in the North or West because they opposed slavery as well as war. Many Quakers in New England, New York, and Pennsylvania were prosperous merchants and traders. They were hit with heavy fines, and when they refused to pay they saw their property confiscated far in excess of the fines. The office of collector was so disagreeable that decent citizens often refused the position. They respected the religious scruples of their pacifist neighbors even if they did not share them. Greedy characters gladly took on the job, grabbing from their victims all they could.

Many Quakers also refused to pay taxes, and several were jailed or had property seized. The majority of the Dunkards, however, appear to have paid taxes.

The Quaker society stood firm against any members making profits out of war. This was a special temptation because many Quakers were merchants. The Friends warned:

Let all be careful not to seek or accept profit by any concern in preparation for war, for how reproachfully inconsistent would it be to refuse an active compliance with warlike measures, and at the same time, not hesitate to enrich ourselves by the commerce and other circumstances dependent on war.

Nathan Trotter, a Quaker millionaire, is but one example of those who refused to buy government bonds because the bonds helped finance the War of 1812. For the small businessman, losses were far harder to take, yet we have the example of the black farmer in New Jersey who had become a Quaker by conviction and who upheld the same principles. He made his living chiefly by selling his produce to workers in a nearby iron foundry. When the foundry began to make cannon for the War of 1812, he stopped selling to the workers because they were making arms, thus risking his livelihood. Unfortunately, his name has not come down to us in the records.

Another principled man of courage whose name we do know was Joseph Hoag. He set out for the South during the war to speak out against both war and slavery. At Knoxville, Tennessee, in the summer of 1813 he found the community in a state of alarm over a threatened Indian invasion. Hoag talked with the commanding general of the troops about the Quaker position on peace. The general was disgusted with local Quakers for refusing to join the muster he had ordered of all able-bodied men, blaming their disobedience on cowardliness. But after listening to

Hoag, he saw the Quakers' sincerity and was willing to help get them exempted.

A man standing nearby overheard the exchange of views and said to Hoag, "Well, stranger, if all the world were of your mind, I would turn in and follow after." To which Hoag at once replied, "Then thou hast a mind to be the last man in the world to be good. I have a mind to be one of the first, and set the rest an example."

Seditious speech and printing were much in evidence during so unpopular a war. Yet President Madison made no attempt to suppress dissent. He was, after all, the author of the First Amendment, guaranteeing to all freedom of speech and the press. He would not push beyond the bounds of his constitutional authority to silence opposition or criticism. As President, he lived up to his principles. He brought the war to an end without infringing a political, civil, or religious right. In future wars, as we shall discover, some presidents did not hesitate to violate the Constitution and curtail civil liberties in order to achieve their goals.

CHAPTER SIX

A Peace Movement Is Born

Sick of the conflict with Britain that ended in 1815, scattered bands of Americans invented a new form of resistance to war. It was the seed of what became known as The Movement during the war in Vietnam.

A leader of this new breed of war resisters was David Dodge (1774–1852). Dodge was a self-taught and self-made man who rose from Connecticut farm boy to prosperous New York merchant. For many years he never questioned the Christian acceptance of war. He trained dutifully with the militia and carried a pistol on his business trips as protection against highway robbery. But one night, at an inn, he nearly shot the landlord, mistaking him for a thief. Horrified at the death he had almost caused, he was led to question how a Christian could carry weapons. For some years he pondered the spirit and meaning of the Gospels in connection with war, and became firmly convinced that wars of all kinds—offensive and defensive—were wrong, as was the use of physical force in self-defense. In pamphlets he published his opposition to the violent method of resisting evil; he would rely only on God's protection from harm. (Not for many years more would the early pacifists explore any other alternative to resisting evil.)

Dodge made out an economic as well as religious case against war. War destroys property, thus doing material harm to the prosperous class; at the same time it inflicts much greater hardship on the poor, who do most of the fighting and who finally pay the cost of war. But rich or poor, no one really gains from war, he said, because war is a waste of man's resources, of God's gifts. Even when an individual or a nation may gain some plunder through war, he went on, they usually lose on the whole more than they gain. Think of the prosperity that would come if all the money spent on war were to go into peaceful enterprise!

Dodge thought too about the biological losses in war. It kills off the young and healthy, the flower of the human race, who enlist because of the touted glamour of military life. The number of widows and orphans are savagely multiplied—the height of inhumanity. And war not only corrupts the morals of soldiers, it leads to a decline in the morality of the whole nation.

Dodge's case against war ranged over a broad ground. He took up the political foolishness of war, calling it self-defeating because it cannot secure what it sets out to achieve—protection against attack; it only raises counterpreparation, leading to international arms races and more and bigger wars. And, he said, the hatred for the enemy whipped up by war and the desire for revenge among the losers leads to an accursed vicious circle from which there is no escape. The difference between aggressive and defensive, or just and unjust wars, Dodge thought ridiculous; they were but tags each side adopted to suit its interests. He showed, too, how war and militarism crippled civil liberties within the nation. As for violent revolution (another form of war) to overthrow tyranny, he found it usually leads to putting a worse tyranny in power.

And what happens to a man's conscience when he wears the uniform of the soldier? It is enslaved to the state. He must kill when ordered. No government, whether democratic or despotic, can allow the soldier to decide what to do according to his conscience. For them to permit that would be to undermine discipline and destroy the power to fight.

Beneath all these arguments showing how wrong war is even from a practical point of view runs Dodge's religious objection. What Christ taught us— to show mercy, to forgive enemies, to put up patiently with oppression, to return only good for evil and love for hatred—all these are opposed to making war. "The whole trade of war," Dodge wrote in his slim book, *War Inconsistent with the Religion of Jesus Christ*, "is returning evil for evil. This is a fundamental principle of the system of self-defense." He could only conclude that the Christian should take no part in war, never, in any way.

Dodge became founder and first president of the New York Peace Society in 1815, the year his book was published. He was the driving force behind the Society for a decade or more. The group started small, with about forty respectable merchants and clergymen. And it stayed small. It tried to attract influential people rather than a mass membership. Its effect was small, too, but it kept the peace flag flying. Within months peace groups formed in other states. The idea leaped the Atlantic and took root in London and Paris.

Dodge would recall how the death of two stepbrothers in the Revolutionary War had nearly driven his mother insane. Noah Worcester, too, was deeply affected by that war. Raised in rural New Hampshire, Worcester (1758–1837) was a veteran of the battle of Bunker Hill. Later he became a Unitarian minister in the Boston area, and was awakened to peace by the strong antiwar sentiment during the War of 1812. He thought that war unnecessary for either side, and unjust for both. In 1814, while the war was still on, he wrote a pamphlet that is a living classic in peace literature. *A Solemn Review of the Custom of War*, he called it, and in it he urged Christians to organize antiwar societies and to work to establish an international system for settling disputes peaceably.

Much of what Worcester said is still valid. He called for immediate action if war was ever to be abolished. In each country peace societies were needed to pressure their governments to follow a conciliatory foreign policy and to spread peace literature among the people. Both school and church are vital to this work, he said, and he pleaded for other churches to stand with the Quakers and the peace sects in their antiwar work.

Between Dodge and Worcester, the foundations were laid for the first organization of peace activists that the world saw. Dodge stressed the personal refusal of the Christian man of peace to have anything

to do with war. Worcester agreed with personal conscientious objection, but he saw the real enemy as
the institution of international war. This "custom
of war" must be challenged and finally eliminated.
Civilized peoples could settle their international disputes by arbitration and a world court.

In 1815, soon after his book appeared, Worcester
and his friends started the Massachusetts Peace Society. Its members were leaders in community life who
saw their task as shaping public opinion toward
peace. One action they took was to petition the state
legislature against compulsory military service for
those conscripts opposed to it. They also wanted
to widen the exemption beyond Quaker objectors
to anyone who believed war to be inconsistent with
Christianity. They failed to convince the lawmakers.

When Worcester invited ex-President John Adams
to join the peace group, Adams refused, giving the
negative reasons so many hold even today:

*Experience has convinced me that wars are as necessary and
as inevitable in our system as hurricanes, earthquakes and volca-
noes. . . . Instead of discouraging a martial spirit, in my opinion it ought to be excited. We have not enough of it to defend
us by sea or land. Universal and perpetual peace appears to
me no more nor less than everlastingly passive obedience and
non-resistance. The human flock would soon be fleeced and butch-*

ered by one or a few. I cannot therefore, Sir, be a subscriber or a member of your society.

From the members of these early peace groups came many works on pacifism, works that explored all sides of the question. They pointed out the close connection between the pursuit of wealth and the way of violence. Wars rarely are fought for the protection of the life and liberty of a nation's citizens. More often than not they turn out to be a sordid business of profit making, though likely to be waged under the banner of "national honor."

One pamphleteer tackled the issue of what would happen to a nation if it decided to disarm regardless of what other nations did. The common view then (and now!) was that such a nation "would be liable to insult, degradation, oppression and subjugation," wrote the Rev. Samuel Whelpley of New York. But he believed that argument would not stand up under close examination. First, he said, such a nation, before saying it was giving up the use of armed force, would take steps to settle its grievances with other nations and thus remove the main causes of future war. But more important would be the vast moral influence the giving up of force would have. The whole world would say, "These people make no war: they even refuse to shed blood in their own defense;

their dealings are just and honorable; they live in peace; they injure nobody; and shall we invade and seek to destroy them? God forbid!" If that nation declared for peace and nonresistance, she would soon be joined by others.

That was optimism, but in a time when many believed human progress was inevitable. Whelpley predicted that other nations would join in establishing a supranational court to settle disputes peacefully. And even if a pacifist nation might be invaded by a power-hungry enemy and conquered, had not this often been the fate of nations armed to the teeth? He drew up a balance sheet between the policy of unilateral disarmament and the pursuit of security through armaments. On the one side was what he thought to be only a remote possibility of the invasion of a disarmed nation. On the other hand, the inevitable outcome: war between nations prepared for war. And this meant the vast destruction of life among both soldiers and civilians, the vast expenses of war, and the aftermath of human suffering lasting many decades. So, on these grounds of both practicality and Christianity, he believed unilateral disarmament to be the best policy.

Nearly fifty local peace groups appeared in those years, and in 1828 many of them merged into the new American Peace Society. Its guiding spirit was

William Ladd (1778–1841), a retired New England sea captain. Born to wealth, and a Harvard graduate, he had experienced a religious conversion that turned him to the peace cause. He was a hearty speaker and tireless campaigner, traveling widely, circulating literature, offering prizes for peace essays, helping to form student peace societies on many campuses. He, too, believed that the age of barbarism had passed. The decline of the slave trade and the growth of the abolition movement he took as signs of progressive human enlightenment.

For the peace seekers the first job was to convert public opinion, "for the continuance of war rests *entirely* on that," said Ladd. His American Peace Society was the first secular peace organization of national scope. It took in state and local societies and welcomed individual members, too. The APS promoted negotiation, arbitration, and especially the idea of a congress of nations to settle all disputes. Members criticized American expansionist policy and argued for disarmament. But their greatest effort went into establishing a world court.

In its campaigns against war, the APS dealt mainly with wars of aggression. It avoided the question of whether "defensive" wars were justifiable because its members were so divided on that point. That reluctance to take a stand against all state and per-

William Lloyd Garrison, the antislavery editor, also organized against all wars, defensive as well as offensive, and all preparations for war. A militant nonresistant, he refused to compromise on vital issues like slavery and war.

sonal use of violence was what led William Lloyd Garrison (1805–1879) and others to form the New England Non-Resistance Society in 1838.

Such problems troubled peace seekers then, as they do now. A modern historian of the peace reform movement, Prof. Charles De Benedetti, poses the crucial questions:

What should be the first object of peace seeking: conversion of the individual human heart, or comprehensive social reformation? What defined the enemy: international war, collective violence, or all forms of coercion? What was the role of a peace movement: to join like-minded reformers in a broad coalition, or to prepare a purified party of believers for radical peace action?

If anyone could be called a "purist," it was Garrison. In great contrast to all the older peace leaders but Dodge, he was born poor and had been a cobbler's and a cabinetmaker's apprentice in boyhood. Then the printer's trade gave him the chance for self-education. All on fire because he hated the sin of slavery, he had founded the New England Anti-Slavery Society in 1831 and made the *Liberator* its official voice. Not content to wait for gradual emancipation, the Garrisonians were pledged to immediate freedom for the slave, by peaceful and lawful means. Never one to soften his criticism, Garrison

77

had been jailed for seven weeks when he called a Massachusetts shipowner a "highway robber and murderer" because he carried slave cargoes. Swiftly the tall, lean firebrand had earned a reputation as a fierce fighter for his beliefs. And now he was as impatient with the gradualism of the peace societies and the Quakers as he was with those who called for black freedom—"but all in good time."

There was much overlap in the membership of the reform societies, and many peace advocates belonged to abolitionist groups as well. The moderate views of William Ladd failed to satisfy Garrison. When he founded the new peace society, he stated its sweeping aims boldly:

We register our testimony, not only against all war, whether offensive or defensive, but all preparation for war;—against every naval ship, every arsenal, every fortification; against the militia system and a standing army; against all military chieftains and soldiers; against all monuments commemorative of victory over a foreign foe, all trophies won in battle, all celebrations in honor of military or naval exploits; against all appropriations for the defense of a nation by force and arms, on the part of any legislative body; against every edict of government, requiring of its subjects military service. Hence, we deem it unlawful to bear arms, or to hold a military office.

*   *   *

A key point in the platform of the nonresistants was the belief that Christian pacifists could take no part in any of the actions of government as it then functioned. Although the Quakers had lost their faith in politics and tried to separate themselves from its corruption, most still voted and some sat in legislatures or held other offices. A majority still believed it was possible to so organize for protection of society that armed force would not be necessary.

But there was a minority of Quakers who, like the Mennonites, rejected any part in civil government, even when military matters were not involved. These might be taken as the Quaker left wing: some of them joined the new Garrison society. In fact, the first president of the nonresistants was the Quaker Effingham L. Capron. The distinguished Philadelphia Quaker Lucretia Mott was drawn to the militancy of the nonresistants and to their refusal to compromise on vital issues like slavery and war. Once she said, "I have no idea, because I am a Non-Resistant, of submitting tamely to injustice inflicted either on me or the slave. I will oppose it with all the moral powers with which I am endowed."

Garrison was raised by his Baptist mother, who soaked his mind in the Bible. His reading of the New Testament convinced him all connection with war was a sin. In Boston he refused service in the militia but did pay a fine. Shortly after, he declared he would "never obey any order to bear arms, but rather cheerfully suffer imprisonment and persecution. What is the design of militia musters? To make men *skilful murderers.* I cannot answer to become a pupil in this sanguinary school."

In the next years Garrison extended nonviolence to include the renunciation of civil government altogether. The logical outcome of Christian pacifism for him was political anarchism. He rejected all man-made law and civil government as unnecessary. If people let themselves be guided by the voice of God within them, they needed no government by either church or state.

Garrison opposed not only international war but all forms of human coercion. The historic peace churches had long stood for passive nonresistance. Garrison's society advanced from that into *active* nonresistance. "We mean to *apply* our principles," as one member put it.

No wonder that the New England press hollered and bellowed at Garrison and his society. "A fanatic" they called him, for he dared to go not only beyond the usual Christian pacifism but to defy the right of state power to exercise coercive authority over the citizenry. Some of Garrison's friends accepted his radical pacifism but not his antigovernment notions. With its extreme and mostly negative views, the society could not unite all absolute pacifists. The dissenters continued to do their work elsewhere.

Going beyond a personal way to live by nonresistance, some reformers tried to create model communities, utopias whose peaceable social behavior would demonstrate how practical this kind of cooperative living was. William Ladd made special efforts to recruit women to the peace cause. "Men make war," he said; "let women make peace." He urged women to rear children without using force, to form female peace societies, and, above all, to press the Christian church to act for peace. Women did become almost a majority of the APS's following. When the Garrison society was founded, several energetic and talented women took part in the first convention and did much to move it on. Among them were Lydia Maria Child, one of the most popular writers of the time; the abolitionist Maria Weston Chapman; and Abby Kelley, the fiery Quaker. Their active role in a time when there was a powerful prejudice against women speaking to mixed audiences of men and women raised the "women's rights" issue; within a few years it would split the abolitionist movement.

The APS drive for a congress of nations bore fruit in 1843, when the first international peace congress met in London. Over three hundred delegates gathered to exchange experiences and coordinate efforts to build international support for peace. The congress urged that all international agreements include a clause requiring the use of arbitration to settle disputes. Five years later Americans joined in a second such congress in Europe, and in three more in the following years. They were signs that true international cooperation against war was a growing movement.

Here in America the APS operated like a modern volunteer peace organization. It gathered information, educated the public in diverse ways, and focused popular pressure on behalf of the peaceful resolution of conflicts. One of its leaders, the brilliant Boston lawyer Charles Sumner (1811–1874), caused a great stir in 1845 when he gave a Fourth of July speech pleading for the United States to give up the false lure of military glory and seek a true grandeur in peace. He boldly chose a military celebration to condemn war and the "heathen patriotism" that sustained it. His case against war was independent of religion; he relied instead on economic and humanitarian arguments. His passionate speech made him the most prominent peace spokesman of the 1840s.

But within a year, the United States would plunge into a war that would split both the country and the peace movement.

CHAPTER SEVEN

This Damnable Mexican War

When Charles Sumner gave his great plea for peace in 1845, he could see America was on the brink of war. Texas had just been annexed by Congress, and Mexico had broken off diplomatic relations with the United States.

Behind the impending conflict lay the issue of slavery. The Mexican republic had opened the rich lands of Texas to colonization in the 1820s. Southerners moved in to cultivate cotton with black slaves. When Mexico ended slavery in 1829, Texans fought a war with her and set up an independent republic. They asked for annexation to the United States, but the abolitionists opposed it. They saw it as a maneuver of slaveholders to extend their system westward.

They feared the vast Texas plains would be carved up into several slave states, adding still more political power to the South. The Mexican government threatened war if annexation went through.

In Congress, John Quincy Adams led the fight against annexation. This country must not grow by conquest, he said. His was an early voice in the movement against American expansionism. As the Mexican fever mounted to its crisis, the true issue was clouded by fervent appeals to nationalism. It was our "manifest destiny" to spread over the whole continent, the nationalists claimed.

In January 1846 President James Polk ordered General Zachary Taylor to move American troops into Mexican territory near the border. When the Mexicans fired the "useful shot" in self-defense, Polk declared that a state of war existed. His Democratic majority allowed the Congress only two hours to debate a war bill, stampeding Congress into hasty action. "The passing of the war bill," wrote Polk's biographer, Charles G. Sellers, "was a striking demonstration of a determined President's ability to compel a reluctant Congress to support a jingoistic foreign policy."

Many in Congress who were against the war, and even spoke up, in the end voted aye. Why? Horace Greeley in his *New York Tribune* had an explanation.

Calling his editorial "Our Country, Right or Wrong!" he wrote:

This is the spirit in which a portion of the Press, which admits that our treatment of Mexico has been ruffianly and piratical, and that the invasion of her territory by Gen. Taylor is a flagrant outrage, now exhorts our People to rally in all their strength, to lavish their blood and treasure in the vindictive prosecution of War on Mexico. We protest against such counsel. . . .

People of the United States! Your Rulers are precipitating you into a fathomless abyss of crime and calamity! Why sleep you thoughtless on the verge, as though this was not your business, or Murder could be hid from the sight of God by a few flimsy rags called banners? Awake and arrest the work of butchery ere it shall be too late to preserve your souls from the guilt of wholesale slaughter!

Antislavery people were enraged by the high-handed way the country had been thrust into war. "If I were a Mexican," shouted Ohio's Tom Corwin to the House, "I would greet you with bloody hands and welcome you to hospitable graves!" Some antislavery Whigs, like young Abraham Lincoln, voted supplies for the war while accusing Polk of starting it in violation of the Constitution. Back home in Illinois, where support for the war ran high, Congressman Lincoln's constituents called him "the Benedict Arnold of our district" and made this his first and last term in Congress.

But other Congressmen refused to vote supplies and men. One of them was Ohio's Joshua Giddings, a frontier lawyer with the torso and temper of a fighting bull. He told the House:

This war is waged against an unoffending people, without just or adequate cause, for the purposes of conquest; with the design to extend slavery; in violation of the Constitution, against the dictates of justice, of humanity, the sentiments of the age in which we live, and the precepts of the religion we profess. I will lend it no aid, no support whatever. I will not bathe my hands in the blood of the people of Mexico, nor will I participate in the guilt of those murders which have been, and which will hereafter be committed by our army there. For these reasons I shall vote against the bill under consideration, and all others calculated to support this war.

It was easy to conceal the facts and call this a "defensive" war once the shooting started. When news of American blood shed by Mexicans arrived, men responded by the thousands to the call for volunteers. While the Northern states contributed comparatively far fewer troops, in the South they overfulfilled the quota set for each state and community; there was no need to draft men to fill the ranks.

Press and public tend to accept a war if it is "short and sweet"—that is, costs little in blood and money, and ends in victory. Many people accepted this war at first. But as the toll in battle and from disease mounted, a growing anger against the war was fueled. Indeed, within a few months, the mood began to shift. The abolitionists, who from the beginning had resisted the war on moral grounds, spoke to more receptive ears. Some religious groups, too—the Quakers, the Unitarians, the Congregationalists—had all along opposed the war. The preacher William H. Channing had even said that if he had to fight in this "damnable war," it would be on the side of the Mexicans.

The American Peace Society voiced its opposition through a steady stream of pamphlets; it spoke for many in New England, where antiwar protest was sharpest and enlistments were smallest. While the Boston minister Theodore Parker (1810–1860) was against the war, too, he believed American rule over the whole continent was inevitable. But he would rather expansion took place peaceably, "by the steady advance of a superior race . . . by commerce, trade, arts . . . by anything rather than bullets." Although a staunch opponent of slavery, Parker held racist views.

His friend Garrison did not agree. "I desire to see human life at all times held sacred," he wrote,

but, in a struggle like this, so horribly unjust and offensive on our part, so purely one of self-defense against lawless invaders on the part of the Mexicans—I feel as a matter of justice, to desire the overwhelming defeat of the American troops, and the success of the injured Mexicans.

His words foreshadowed how Garrison and other nonresistants would modify their views during the next decade, as circumstances changed. They would come to accept the use of violence when they thought it would advance the cause of freedom.

In July 1846, as American troops were advancing in Mexico, Henry David Thoreau (1817–1862) was jailed in Concord. Years before he had refused to pay his poll tax to support a government that sanctioned slavery and was now fighting a war to extend it. Thoreau's going to jail was his way of showing that a man of conscience had a right to resist his government when it did wrong. Brief as his prison hours were—he stayed in jail only overnight, until someone paid his taxes without his permission—they led to his most influential essay, on civil disobedience. It reached only a handful in its first form, a lecture, but in print it proved to have a universal

Henry David Thoreau was jailed in 1846 for refusing to pay taxes to support the war against Mexico. His powerful essay "Civil Disobedience" urged conscientious objectors to carry actions of protest far enough to correct injustices.

appeal. What it says goes beyond the Mexican War and the slavery struggle with which it was immediately concerned. Thoreau spoke to the issue of the moral law in conflict with government law. The law is not to be respected merely because it is the law, but only because it is right and just. If unjust laws exist, civil disobedience is an effective way to oppose and change them, he said.

Thoreau's was a radical view of conscientious objection. The religious pacifists taught that a person must *refrain* from certain actions that went against his conscience. Thoreau urged that each citizen had an *obligation to disobey* any law that would violate that conscience. By refusing to pay taxes, by going to jail if necessary, and thus clogging the government's machinery, a man could awaken the citizens to a wrong and make them willing to correct it. Thoreau believed that a conscientious objector, the person he called "a majority of one," might take a position against war or injustice on secular grounds.

This was a considerable step beyond the quietism of some peace sects. Thoreau shaped a different code of behavior. He wanted the man of conscience to carry action far enough to *change* society. Don't just stand aside from injustice or war, he was saying; do something! If that meant breaking an unjust law or refusing to bear arms and going to prison, he was willing to do it.

Thoreau's expression of the doctrine of civil disobedience would move people around the world to practice it against war and against tyranny. Seventy years later Mahatma Gandhi developed satyagraha, a concept that organized nonviolent action into mass moral pressure for the gaining of social and political goals. Thoreau's civil disobedience was one of Gandhi's main tools for winning independence for India without bringing about a bloody war between the Indians and the occupying British. Martin Luther King in the 1950s would respond in his way to the words uttered in Concord long before.

The Quakers, of course, condemned the Mexican War like any other. But they were even more outspoken than usual because they detested the aggressive foreign policy of Polk and the threatened extension of the slave system. The Friends' testimony on the war carried undertones of political protest. This was a "barbarous" war, they said publicly, "an atrocity," a "horrid affair." To show their disapproval, Friends were asked not only to give no sanction to military laws but to vote against anyone in favor of the war and to petition Congress to put a stop to it.

The Non-Resistant Society did little during the war. Too much of its energy went into endless debate on theoretical issues. It is hard to find evidence of much antiwar action. By abstaining from any connection with politics, they were left with no influence. Without nonresistant help, the antiwar forces in Massachusetts got the legislature to urge "all good citizens to join the efforts to arrest this war." In New Hampshire a resolution against the war was adopted by the legislature and signed by the governor. The mounting public impatience with the war altered the political climate and frustrated Polk. He gave up his hope of grabbing all of Mexico and was forced to accept a more limited conquest. The antiwar movement thus helped to contain the violence and cut short the bloodletting.

One peace seeker of those years broke new ground in resisting war. He was Elihu Burritt (1810–1879), one of the most remarkable Americans of the nineteenth century. He founded the first secular pacifist organization to rally workers and farmers to fight against war. His League of Universal Brotherhood, created in 1847 during the Mexican War, was also the first secular peace group to organize internationally.

Burritt, born in poverty, the son of a cobbler, had an unquenchable thirst for learning and for helping humanity. Denied schooling, he was apprenticed as a boy to the village blacksmith and made smithing his lifelong trade. With no one's help he acquired a working knowledge of some forty languages. If reaching out to other peoples is a path to peace,

Elihu Burritt, the "Learned Blacksmith," pioneered many techniques—the peace pledge, mass demonstrations, strikes—to rally people in America and abroad against any kind of war.

none was better equipped for it than the many-tongued Burritt. His great intelligence and strength of character enabled him to master many fields of knowledge. While still a young man, he gave ardent support to a wide range of humanitarian causes. He never stopped thinking of himself as an artisan and devoted himself to whatever would benefit the working class. He continued to work at the forge long after he had won fame as "the Learned Blacksmith."

What prompted Burritt to pacifism? In his study of the sciences he was struck with wonder at the oneness of the universe and all its phenomena, including humankind. Violence ran counter to the "perfect symmetry" of God's work and the law of love. This insight led him to devote himself to halting the mutual murder of people when nations go to war.

With his enthusiasm and talent, Burritt was eagerly welcomed into the American Peace Society and soon became the editor of its organ, the *Advocate of Peace*. But when he failed to win the APS to a total renunciation of war, including defensive wars, he withdrew to form his own society. It was on a peace mission to England that he set up the League of Universal Brotherhood on a platform of absolute pacifism. The League gathered in members from America, England, and several countries on the Continent. Burritt published both a weekly peace paper and a popular monthly from Worcester, Massachusetts, where he had long lived. It was artisans and farmers who made up the vast majority of the League's members during the ten years it lasted.

In Burritt's view, more was needed to end war than appeals to politicians and opinion makers. The peace reform must be carried to the masses. He wanted to remove "the spirit of war from the hearts of the people." And to do that he developed many of the most effective modern publicity methods.

Even before the Mexican War, when a dispute over Oregon's boundaries threatened war between Britain and America, Burritt came up with a useful approach. He got a few English friends to work with him in launching an exchange of "Friendly Addresses" between English and American cities linked by place name or similar industries. These urged one another's working people not to be lured into a war to enrich the "aristocracy, our enemies and yours." Such proofs of antiwar sentiment were presented to political leaders in both nations.

From the temperance movement he adapted the idea of a pledge of abstinence from any kind of war. Some fifty thousand English and American war resisters signed the peace pledge:

Believing all war to be inconsistent with the spirit of Christianity, and destructive to the best interests of mankind, I do hereby pledge myself never to enlist or enter into any army or navy, or to yield any voluntary support or sanction to the preparation for or prosecution of any war, by whomsoever, for whatsoever proposed, declared, or waged. And I do hereby associate myself with all persons, of whatever country, condition, or color, who have signed, or shall hereafter sign this pledge, in a "League of Universal Brotherhood"; whose object shall be to employ all legitimate and moral means for the abolition of all war and all spirit, and all the manifestation of war, throughout the world; for the abolition of all restrictions upon international correspondence and friendly intercourse, and of whatever else tends to make enemies of nations, or prevents their fusion into one peaceful brotherhood; for the abolition of all institutions and customs which do not recognize the image of God and a human brother in every man of whatever clime, color, or condition of humanity.

Peace fairs were held to raise funds for placing the pledge and other antiwar messages in scores of newspapers. Burritt proposed an international workers' parliament as a means of achieving peace and called for workers of the world to unite in a strike whenever war threatened.

Early in 1848, a peace treaty with Mexico was signed. By the agreement the United States acquired 850,000 square miles, about one-third of Mexico's land. It was more than the combined area of France,

Spain, and Italy. The United States had grown enormously through its aggression. The dissent expressed during the war revealed the sectional conflicts that had begun to strain the bonds of union and to break apart both major parties.

How would the new territories be organized? Would they be open to free labor alone? Or would the Southerners have an equal chance to bring in their slaves, against whom free labor could not compete?

These were basic questions, questions not settled by the war, but opened up by it.

CHAPTER EIGHT

To Choose Between Two Evils

As 1850 came in, a showdown seemed near between antislavery and proslavery forces. Both sides recognized that the country had reached a turning point. The Union was divided evenly—fifteen slave states and fifteen free. Slavery was entwined with every public question of the day. Southern editors threatened secession if slavery were interfered with in any way, while the Northern press warned that the Union would be torn apart if slavery were not checked.

In Congress a great debate took place over three decisive issues: slavery in the territories, slavery and the slave trade in the District of Columbia, and the fugitive slaves who were finding shelter in the Northern states. It ended in the adoption of a group of bills proposed by Senator Henry Clay of Kentucky. Through the Compromise of 1850, as it was called, Texas was brought into the Union as a slave state, California as a free state. The slave trade was abolished in the District of Columbia, and a new and harsher fugitive slave law was passed to force Northerners to return runaways to their owners. Central to the compromise was a "popular sovereignty" provision that said that when a territory came into the Union as a state, it would enter with or without slavery as its constitution prescribed at the time of admission.

Most Americans hailed the compromise as a final settlement of the question. They hoped it would mean peace in their time. But Clay himself admitted that it was more a Southern victory than a compromise. And the radical Republican congressman Thaddeus Stevens said this "compromise" will become "the fruitful mother of future rebellion, disunion and civil war."

It happened almost at once. Violence erupted in Kansas between the free-labor forces and slaveholders, each side trying to sway the territory their way. The plains of Kansas became a bloody battleground. In the North, abolitionists defied the Fugitive Slave Law by helping to rescue runaways, many times resorting to force. Pacifists who had never thought they would abandon their beliefs found themselves yielding to the passionate temper of the times. They raised money to buy supplies and weapons for the antislavery settlers in Kansas, and some joined mobs who stormed courthouses and jails to liberate captured fugitives.

What solution could pacifists offer for these immediate crises? When revolution exploded all across Europe in 1848 in the name of freedom and national independence, peace lovers felt deep sympathy for the oppressed seeking to break their chains. But they condemned even indirect aid to violence. The American Margaret Fuller (1810–1850), working in a hospital for Italian rebels, wrote friends back home who criticized her for aiding the rebels: "What you say about the Peace way is deeply true," she admitted;

if any one sees clearly how to work in that way, let him, in God's name! Only, if he abstains from fighting giant wrongs, let him be sure he is really ardently at work undermining them, or, better still, sustaining the rights that are to supplant them. Meanwhile, I am not sure that I can keep my hands free from blood.

Like Fuller, nonresistant Samuel J. May (1797–1871) looked with favor on the revolutionary political and social movements of his time. He mourned when the Poles' fight against tsarist oppression failed, but he regretted that Poland "sought her deliverance by an appeal to arms." The outcome of the Polish uprising illustrated the futility of killing in however just a cause. "War is not the means appointed by our heavenly Father for the redress of any of our grievances," he said. There had to be a better way to overcome evil.

One after another the imprisoned nations made bids for their freedom—Italians, Germans, Poles, Hungarians, Serbs, Greeks. But all went down to defeat. Their leaders fled into exile, some seeking support in America, where they preached war and revolution to liberate their people. The pacifists did not disagree with their aims, only with the means they chose to achieve their ends. To Garrison's circle, nonviolent resistance seemed the true path to take. To the Hungarian nationalist Kossuth, Garrison wrote that he joined with him in condemning Austrian domination, "but the lessons of vengeance which thou art teaching thy countrymen are such as to degrade and brutalize humanity. Tell the Hungarians that a bloody warfare to maintain their nationality is incompatible with moral greatness and Christian love."

The American peace movement dimmed as national politics flared into fiery quarrels over slavery.

When Charles Sumner criticized slaveholders on the Senate floor, a Southern congressman caned him savagely. Members of the Congress wore guns openly as they went about their lawmaking.

Then, in October 1859, John Brown led twenty-one men in an attack upon the federal arsenal at Harpers Ferry, Virginia. It was an attempt to spark a massive slave uprising and carry emancipation through the South by the sword. Though it failed, the raid gave a new direction to events. John Brown had shown there were men who would do more than moralize against slavery. How many other John Browns were arming themselves to follow his example?

When men like Ralph Waldo Emerson spoke up and called John Brown "a new saint who will make the gallows as glorious as the cross," it was a sign to the South that behind the man they called a fanatic was a vast public spirit that approved what he had done. The peace advocate Lydia Maria Child wrote that the raid on Harpers Ferry seemed a mad attempt:

According to my views such violent attempts to right wrong are both injudicious and evil. But Captain Brown takes the Old Testament view of things. He is a real psalm-singing, praying Puritan, of the old stamp. Of course, it is simple justice to judge him from his own conscientious point of view. If we praise Concord Fight, where men fought for their own rights, how can we consistently blame this far more disinterested effort for the freedom of others? Deeply as I regret the whole affair, I cannot help honoring the brave old man.

Mrs. Child was calling John Brown's use of force wrong in one sentence while finding words to praise him in the next.

Her inconsistency typified the confused feeling of many of the pacifists. Some drifted into political passivity, but others shifted to the acceptance of violence when it promised to advance emancipation. For example, among John Brown's men at Harpers Ferry were two young Quakers from Iowa, the brothers Edwin and Barclay Coppoc; raised in the way of nonviolence, they had chosen to use force if it could win freedom for the slave.

Angelina Grimké, abolitionist and Quaker, said that reformers had "to choose between two evils, and all that we can do is to take the *least,* and baptize liberty in blood, if it must be so." The Rev. Samuel May publicly admitted that violence was needed to bring about emancipation.

On the day of his execution, John Brown scrawled

on a piece of paper he handed to his jailer, "I, John Brown, am now quite certain that the crimes of this guilty land will never be purged away but with blood. I had, as I now think vainly, flattered myself that without very much bloodshed it might be done." And from Garrison, the nonresistant, came these words: "In firing his gun John Brown has merely told us what time of day it is. It is high noon, thank God!"

A year after John Brown was hanged, Abraham Lincoln was elected President. His victory broke the long rule of slave power. As he waited to take office, most of the Southern states seceded, seizing federal forts and arsenals and drawing up plans to establish themselves as an independent nation. Most Americans, North and South, dreaded war and hoped some compromise could be reached to keep the peace. But abolitionists stood solid against making any concessions on slavery. Let the South go, some argued, and slavery will fade away. Others replied that would mean deserting the slave, leaving him helpless, separated from his friends in the North.

A few weeks after Lincoln took office, the South fired on the besieged federal garrison at Fort Sumter. The Civil War had begun. The attack on Sumter revolutionized public feeling in the North. Overnight a war fever took hold and raged through every

Northern town and village. Young and old, men and women shared in a frenzy of patriotism. Declaring that "insurrection" existed, Lincoln called for seventy-five thousand men to volunteer for three months' service. Few saw that this would be no ninety-day fight but the bloodiest war of the nineteenth century.

Soon after Sumter, the American Peace Society at its annual meeting gave its support to the Union. They got around their peace principles by calling the conflict not a war but a rebellion to be suppressed by the police power of the government. Gerrit Smith, the APS president, said this was really a war to end war, for slavery itself was "the most cruel and horrid form of war." A small minority of the APS would have no part of the war, and Elihu Burritt blamed the APS for not having promoted years ago the scheme of compensated emancipation, which he believed the South would have accepted.

The Garrison group backed the Union cause completely. How could Garrison, ardent advocate of nonviolence, cast aside his principles to support the war? Because he was just as ardently the enemy of slavery. And when the two values he cherished came into opposition, he chose the one above the other. When Lincoln's Emancipation Proclamation made abolition a prime Northern objective, Garrison and the nonresistants were jubilant. Now they could justify their support of the war by reasoning that this was God's way of freeing the slaves. To which some, who did not abandon nonresistance, replied that the end, no matter how noble, never justified such means.

There was opposition to the war in both the North and the South. Conservative Democrats in such states as Ohio and New York sympathized with the South and called for peace. And Unionists in non-slaveholding corners of the Confederacy denounced the rebels for starting a war poor farmers would fight for the planters' benefit. Many who previously refused war taxes decided that to pay them now was all right, because the war's aim was more to free slaves than to kill people. The Quakers were more tolerant of those who paid taxes than before.

Only a handful of the secular peace advocates kept aloft the flag of nonviolence. One veteran of the movement, Joshua Blanchard, a Boston merchant now in his eighties, rebuked the APS for deserting its principles and refusing to try to stop the war. A signer of Burritt's peace pledge, he polled eighty other signers and found that only three had kept the pledge and applied it to *this* war.

In the beginning, the Union relied on the old way of raising an army—by an offer of money. Federal, state, and local governments offered bounties to join up. The quality of volunteers was poor. General Grant complained that it took eight bounties to get one good soldier. By 1863, with the war dragging on and enlistments unsatisfactory, the Congress adopted the first national draft of able-bodied males twenty to forty-five years old. Local districts were assigned a quota of men per draft call, to be filled by volunteers, paid substitutes, or draftees. No exemption was made for conscientious objectors, but they were allowed for the mentally ill, sole supporters of aged or widowed parents, and those possessed of certain physical disabilities. Exemptions ran so high that 70 percent of the men called in the first draft escaped in this way.

But men could avoid service, too, by paying a fee or providing a substitute. After a huge number of those called up got out of it by paying a fee, that escape hatch was closed; substitution was obviously more productive for the government. Those acceptable as substitutes had to have been ineligible for the draft. They got as much as $1,000 to serve in another's place, a very large sum of money in those days.

The Confederacy passed its first draft law in April 1862. It exempted a great many occupations, which made fraud easy. In addition, none of those exempted were required to pay commutation fees. Later that year a law exempted Friends, Nazarenes, Mennonites, and Dunkards—but only if they would furnish substitutes or pay a tax of $500. As Confederate losses in the war mounted, the number of exemptions was sharply slashed, and the provision for COs was cut out altogether.

Resistance to the draft boiled up all across the Union. A Northern journalist, Joel Headley, wrote that conscription was seen to be "a tyrannical, despotic, unjust measure—an act which has distinguished tyrants the world over and should never be tolerated by a free people." It was plain at once that the draft favored the rich and hit hardest at the poor. But there were other causes, too, for resentment. The war was becoming more and more unpopular. The quick victory predicted had not happened. Loss of life was enormous. Rising inflation had shrunk what wages could buy. Fear spread that after the war blacks would hurry North to take jobs away from whites.

As soon as the first draft call was made in July 1863, mobs rioted against it in a dozen cities. The worst outbreak hit New York. Shouting antidraft slogans, crowds marched into mid-Manhattan, halting streetcars and cutting telegraph wires until they reached the draft office and burned it down. From the draft the mob shifted its anger to the blacks

and the abolitionists. They burned the Colored Or-
phan Asylum, attacked blacks on the street—shooting, burning, and lynching them—looted the homes
and businesses of blacks and of white abolitionists,
and beat up police, draft officers, and reporters. For
three days the violent fever raged, until ten thousand
federal troops finally stopped it. More than a thousand people were killed or injured. The government
suspended the draft in New York for more than a
month. Frightened by the draft riots, municipal,
state, and federal governments earmarked considerable funds to subsidize poor draftees who could not
otherwise afford to buy their way out of service
by paying for substitutes.

As in most wars, few men were burning to fight.
They fought if they were forced to, or paid to. Men
ducked the draft or resisted it openly. They refused
to register, did not show up for induction, destroyed
draft records, deserted, fled to Canada. (Hundreds
of thousands failed to register for the draft, 160,000
failed to appear for induction, and 260,000 deserted.) Directly, the draft brought in scarcely 6 percent of the 2 million men in the Union Army. It
was substitution and bounties that filled the ranks,
largely with poor men. They served mostly for pay,
not patriotism, but it was enough for the Union to
win the war.

The peace churches clung grimly to their pacifist

convictions throughout the long war. Everywhere the Yearly Meetings of the Quakers refused to disavow their principles when it came to conscription or any other demand for support of either side in the war.

Since no provision was made in the draft law for conscientious objectors, the Quakers felt they could not rely on state militia laws for protection, so they pressed Congress for action. In February 1864 Congress voted the first alternative service law in American history. It permitted COs to perform hospital work or to care for freedmen as a legitimate substitute for army service, or to pay a fee of $300. No allowance was made, however, for refusal to cooperate in any way, which caused the peace sects many hardships. Quakers, Shakers, Brethren in Christ, Rogerenes, and other absolutist pacifists were penalized for abiding by their beliefs.

Throughout the war, Quakers offered counsel and care to their young members of draft age. They set up special committees to help COs state their cases to the draft board, to keep in touch with those arrested for noncompliance and placed in prison or military camps, and to negotiate with the authorities, civil or military.

As in earlier wars, most Quakers refused to pay another to fight in their place. "If it is wrong for me to fight and kill my fellow-creature," wrote one Friend, "it must be wrong to pay my money to hire another to do it; just as it would be to hire a man to steal or murder."

If nonresistants in the peace societies were swept from their pacifist moorings by a war to free the slaves, so, too, were many young Quakers. Although reared in Quaker homes, they decided to go against the discipline of their church and fight. They chose to act upon another Quaker principle—resistance to oppression. The Coppoc brothers who fought alongside John Brown set them an example.

The number who took up arms revealed that for many of the young, the pacifist belief had lost the vitality it had had for earlier generations. The usual disownment process was generally postponed till the war's end because the Friends sympathized so strongly with the cause their young men fought for. If the returning soldiers showed a renewed trust in the peace testimony, they were received back lovingly.

In defense of their highest beliefs, about fifteen hundred men sought CO status in the Civil War. Their treatment by the authorities ranged from leniency to brutal punishment. Objectors in the North usually met little hardship. President Lincoln and his Secretary of War, Edwin Stanton, understood the Quaker position. Lincoln let them spread peace tracts freely, even among the troops—perhaps because it was widely realized that the Quakers opposed the war as the wrong means to an end they supported, and not out of hidden sympathy for the enemy's cause. Both Lincoln and Stanton did what they could to prevent persecution for matters of conscience.

COs in the South had a harder time, partly because the Confederacy was so short of manpower and less familiar with the pacifist viewpoint. In both North and South, the officer class was harsher to pacifists than the men in the ranks were. Although no noncombatants were executed, many died from their poor treatment by the army.

Very few Southern Quakers volunteered for the Confederate Army because their church was not only pacifist but antislavery. Some young men escaped North to avoid the draft, while others hid in forests or caves. Some remained at home to await the authorities, and still others paid the commutation fee of $500 permitted by the Confederacy.

COs who came under Southern military command were often treated cruelly by zealous junior officers out to break their spirit and force them to accept combat duty. They were pierced with bayonets, hung by the thumbs, beaten, kicked, gagged with open bayonets, deprived of sleep, kept on a bread and water diet, penned in filthy cells, denied the means to wash themselves. Often they were threatened with shooting or hanging. Many COs were forced to march into combat zones with their rifles bound to their backs. The men who would not give in were sometimes kept in army camps or prisons for several years, freed only when the Confederacy collapsed.

The extraordinary steadfastness of one Southern Quaker has come down to us in a report of the Friends' fate under Confederate rule. Seth W. Laughlin was a man with a wife and seven children when he joined the Society of Friends in Virginia during the war. As a CO he refused military service, was arrested in 1863, and taken to a military camp near Petersburg, Virginia. This is what happened to him:

First they kept him without sleep for 36 hours, a soldier standing by with a bayonet to pierce him, should he fall asleep. Finding that this did not overcome his scruples, they proceeded for three hours each day to buck him down. He was then suspended by the thumbs for an hour and a half. This terrible ordeal was passed through with each day for a week. Then, thinking him conquered, they offered him a gun; he was unwilling to use the weapon. Threats, abuse and persecution were alike unavailing, and in desperate anger the Colonel ordered him courtmartialled. After being tried for insubordination he was ordered shot.

Preparations were accordingly made for the execution of this terrible sentence. The army was summoned to witness the scene, and soldiers were detailed. Guns, six loaded with bullets and six without, were handed to twelve chosen men. Seth Laughlin, as calm as any man of the immense number surrounding him, asked time for prayer, which, of course, could not be denied him. The supposition was natural that he wished to pray for himself. But he was ready to meet his Lord and so he prayed not for himself but for them: "Father, forgive them, for they know not what they do."

Strange was the effect of this familiar prayer upon men used to taking human life and under strict military orders. Each man, however, lowered his gun, and they resolutely declared that they would not shoot such a man, thereby braving the result of disobeying military orders. But the chosen twelve were not the only ones whose hearts were touched.

The officers themselves revoked the sentence. He was led away to prison, where for weeks he suffered uncomplainingly from his severe punishments. He was finally sent to Windsor Hospital at Richmond, Virginia, where he was taken very sick, and after a long, severe illness, he passed quietly away. . . .

In the North, Quakers who refused to accept alternate service were drafted into the army. But fairly often on appeal to Secretary Stanton, they were paroled or furloughed for an indefinite period. This kept many of them free from service until the war ended. In the interval between drafting and release from service, however, some COs suffered abuse. An appeal to Stanton for help records that a Massachusetts Quaker was tied up in the woods with mules, suspended by his hands from a pole, deprived of shelter and food, and then put in the guardhouse for nearly two months. All this he took with great courage and patience, though his health was seriously injured.

In the same year that Seth Laughlin was drafted by the Confederates, the Vermont Quaker Cyrus Pringle was drafted into the Union Army. He was an absolutist who refused to bear arms or perform any alternate service. He kept a diary of his sufferings that has been reprinted many times as an inspiration for later war resisters. (Pringle, a self-educated farmer, became renowned as a botanist who collected and classified a thousand species of plants during forty years of research.)

Like Laughlin, Pringle was a recent convert to the Friends. Forced into service, he was sent to an army camp near Boston. There he refused to do any military chores, even to help clean the camp or fetch water. When offered the chance to work in a camp hospital, he refused that, too. He was sent South to the battlegrounds. When he refused on marches to carry a gun and pack, they were strapped forcibly to his back. Under hard treatment and threats of court-martial and shooting, he finally agreed to work in the medical service, which he could see urgently needed help. A great load seemed lifted from him, but soon he felt he had "sold out our Master. That first day was one of the bitterest I experienced." He went back to the colonel and told him he could not set aside his conscience. "No Friend, who is really such, desiring to keep himself clear of complicity with this system of war and to bear a perfect testimony against it, can lawfully perform service in the hospitals of the Army in lieu of bearing arms," he wrote in his diary.

The angry colonel lost patience with his defiance. When Pringle refused to clean his gun, which had rusted yellow, he was punished.

Two sergeants soon called for me, and taking me a little aside, bid me lie down on my back, and stretching my limbs apart, tied cords on my wrists and ankles, and these to four stakes driven in the ground somewhat in the form of an X. I was very quiet in my mind as I lay there on the ground [soaked] with the rain of the previous day, exposed to the heat of the sun and suffering as from sorrow that such things should be in our country. . . . And I was sad, that one endeavoring to follow our dear Master should be so generally regarded as a despicable and stubborn culprit.

This was the last attempt to torture Pringle into submission. Quakers intervened to have Pringle and other COs sent to Washington from the military camps of Virginia. Soon they received their paroles through Lincoln's order, and at last were able to go home.

Other peace sects as well as the utopian communities stood by their pacifist principles during the Civil War. The Shakers held to an absolutist position, which caused the arrest of some of their small membership; when a Shaker delegation went to Lincoln with a request for draft exemption, he granted Shaker draftees an indefinite furlough. All the male members of the Oneida Community in upstate New York refused to fight. The few thousand members of the Mennonites, the Brethren, and the other rural peace sects shared the same wartime experiences as the Quakers. The German peace sects opposed military service and support of a warmaking government. Usually they paid a fee in place of service, but they declined to hire substitutes.

The recent appearance of the "millenarian nonresistants"—such as the Seventh-Day Adventists—complicated the picture. These new-style pacifists refused any part in man's wars so that they might be better prepared to do violence for the Lord on the day of the second coming of Christ—when all the unrighteous would be extinguished. Their conditional acceptance of violence made it hard to define the limits of true conscientious objection.

Adventist pacifists were influenced by their reading of the New Testament and by the Garrisonian nonresistant movement. When the Civil War began, they said they were strongly antislavery. They lived, however, in daily expectation of the end of the world and the accompanying wiping out of the wicked. As followers of Christ, they could not respond to the call to arms in this earthly war. They had to stand aloof from the violence around them.

The Civil War had started with the limited aim of restoring the Union; it ended with the overthrow of slavery. For 4 million blacks the dream of freedom had come true. It was a victory dearly bought. In the proportion of killed and wounded to participants, the Civil War was the costliest the United States had fought. Casualties totaled between 33 and 40 percent of the combined Union and Confederate forces.

In the wake of the human slaughter came the economic costs—enormous taxes, sky-high prices, heavy debts, cheapened currency. Some soldiers who survived the struggle asked why we could not learn to live by reason rather than by war. And civilians who watched the maimed and diseased soldiers return home wondered if their sufferings could not have been spared by some other way to resolve conflict.

General Sheridan predicted ten years after the war that new and more horrible methods of killing would wipe war out of history. Ulysses S. Grant, the Union commander, upon becoming President said that "an arbitration between two nations may not satisfy either party at the time, but it satisfies the conscience of mankind; and it must commend itself more and more as a means of adjusting disputes."

There was another and a more far-reaching side to the Civil War's heritage. In both North and South the martial spirit roused by combat left among many a legacy of unthinking patriotism. People forgot the blood and havoc. They recalled the war through a mist of sentimentality. The popular songs and stories and memoirs about the war passed on to the next generation a romantic faith in the appeal to arms.

CHAPTER NINE

A Splendid Little War

As the country settled into peacetime living, Americans moved into the age of industrialism and empire. The Civil War had transformed the nation's life. Boys and girls born into a nation of farmers, independent craftsmen, and small manufacturers came of age in a society of great capitalists and big factories concentrated in the cities. Railroads tracked across the land, opening up every corner of the country. Millions of immigrants from southern and eastern Europe poured into America. From the Civil War to 1900, the nation's population tripled. The value of production multiplied three times over on the farm and elevenfold in the factory.

One outcome of the great revolution based upon

the machine and the factory was to multiply the poor many times over. In 1890, eleven out of twelve families had an average income of but $380 a year. The richest 1 percent of the country enjoyed wealth greater than the total of the remaining 99 percent. "Never before or since in American history have the rich been richer and the poor so poor," wrote one historian.

The fifty years between the Civil War and the outbreak of World War I were an age of industrial violence. The swift growth of industry and the enormous power of the corporations got beyond society's control. Bloody strikes erupted all over the country when workers were forced to fight for the elementary right to organize and better their conditions. The nineties saw the closing of the frontier, a great depression that made millions jobless, a revolt among embittered farmers and workers ready to try all sorts of radical proposals for ending their troubles. Reformers feared that unless peaceful means of resolving such conflicts were found, society would be torn to pieces.

The answer to the nation's economic crisis for some businessmen and politicians was to find new markets abroad. They looked especially to Latin America, the Caribbean, and Asia. They wanted the opportunity to invest in foreign railroads, mines, and factories. And they expected systematic help from Washington for their economic expansion overseas. Inevitably it meant pushing American power throughout the world.

What the new times demanded of peace seekers was a deeper search into the causes of conflict, both at home and between nations. Was there any way to eliminate the violence rising within America and the military clashes threatened by the new policy of imperialism?

A few of the old-time peace workers carried their principles into the postwar period. Elihu Burritt was alarmed by the arms race in Europe. He saw no signs of any government brave enough to set an example by disarming unilaterally. He turned to the working classes for a solution and called on them to take direct action against war by striking. The very threat of mass demonstrations would, he hoped, pressure the nations to agree to gradual and proportional reductions in their armaments. That idea of direct, nonviolent mass action would be picked up and carried through in the century to come.

Old and worn out by his long struggle for black emancipation, William Lloyd Garrison was more a living monument to radical pacifism than an active leader. But his earlier writings on nonresistance, together with Thoreau's, would influence both Leo

Tolstoy and Gandhi.

The old American Peace Society clung to the traditions of the conservative peace movement. As before, it called for universal and compulsory arbitration of disputes between countries and for the creation of an international court of justice. But relying on businessmen for support, it failed to dig into the economic and social roots of war. It bumbled along into the twentieth century, showing only a few signs of vitality. Its eyes were shut to the violent clashes of labor and capital and it did nothing to halt the wars against the Plains Indians unleashed by Washington.

Outside the peace churches, it was the Universal Peace Union that brought alive again the radical pacifism of the pre-Civil War years. The UPU was founded in 1866 by Alfred Love (1830–1913). A Philadelphia Quaker, he was a prosperous woolens merchant. During the Civil War he refused military service and turned away profitable government contracts. Concerned with many reforms, he led the UPU to campaign in behalf of unjustly treated ethnic groups—the blacks, the Indians, the new immigrants from Europe and Asia. The Union came out for women's rights and for arbitration of labor disputes.

But the UPU built organizations in only four northeastern states and never enrolled over four hundred members, although it could count on another three to four thousand sympathizers for aid and action. It relied on popular conventions, rallies, petitions, the press, the pulpit to promote its platform of complete pacifism. It considered war a sin against God under any circumstances whatever. It always supported conscientious objectors and sought legal recognition of their rights.

The Union saw the link between war and economic injustice. Its leaflets, pamphlets, and journals tried to awaken the public to the truth:

Wars are usually inaugurated by the upper and governing classes for the purpose of personal or national ambition, preferment or pride, and the mutilation, torture and death of men from the lower and laboring classes is less an object of consideration than the money which is required for their equipment and support as soldiers.

About a third of the Union's active members were women, and they included many notable advocates of women's rights—Susan B. Anthony, Lucretia Mott, Belva Lockwood, Lucy Stone, Ernestine Rose. The UPU asserted that women had an especially vital role to play in working for a peaceful world.

When war between France and Germany broke out in 1870, it moved a feminist leader to publish the antiwar "Appeal to Womenhood Throughout the World." Julia Ward Howe urged Christian women everywhere to speak out against war and to call for an international women's peace congress. But she failed to rally enough support. The feminists of that time preferred to focus on temperance and women's suffrage, and the men presiding over an international peace congress in Paris refused to let Howe speak to it.

The Universal Peace Union claimed that war could be ended only if society was reshaped in a spirit of love and brotherhood. International arbitration and a world court of justice were on its agenda, of course. But it went beyond these to oppose military appropriations in Congress, imperialist adventures abroad, and the glorification of war. The Union pleaded for America to open the path to peace by a policy of unilateral disarmament. It attacked the militarization of young people, opposing military drill in school or college and the exaltation of war in classroom textbooks.

From the peace churches, however, there came little action for peace. Without the pressure of wartime upon them, they sank into apathy. The Friends were divided by internal issues and failed to develop a program of nonresistance. Their press, however, did discuss the growing militarism and expansionism painfully visible in the United States.

From Friends' meetings came complaints of the folly of piling up arms and appeals even for unilateral disarmament. But pacifism got less attention than other issues that seemed more pressing—temperance, prison reform, Indian rights.

Still, in 1867 some midwestern Quakers formed the Peace Association of Friends in North America. They hoped to tug Friends and others out of the trough of indifference into which the public had dropped in the postwar years. The Association began a monthly journal, *Messenger of Peace*, which would keep going for seventy years. And through reprints it kept alive many of the pioneering peace classics of the prewar generation. It prepared special peace pamphlets for children, telling of the horrors of war and detailing the lives of dedicated peace workers.

After a gap of some forty years, American peace workers helped bring about a universal peace congress in Paris in 1889. It began a new series of European meetings that would expand the peace movement. At home, in 1895, the Quakers Albert and Alfred Smiley opened their resort at Lake Mohonk, New York, to annual summer conferences of national leaders seeking to develop ways to arbitrate international disputes. These continued for twenty-two years, building a broader base for peace activism.

Thus, a small number of American and European activists worked together to shape some kind of mechanism to keep the peace among nations. But their work was stymied by the ideas about racial superiority that dominated social thinking in that era. Racial theories that sprang up in Europe spread rapidly in America. The new pseudo-science held the "Nordic" or "Aryan" stock to be superior, and other peoples, especially those of darker color—black, brown, red, yellow—were looked down upon, were fit only to serve this master race. And the superiors, like the old slavemasters, were expected to show a paternal concern for their inferiors, to look after them and make all their decisions for them.

This white racism blended with economic pressures for building an American empire abroad. The shapers of foreign policy believed the nation had to compete aggressively for wealth and power if it was to survive and progress. They saw the world as divided into superior white people and inferior darker people. The "uncivilized" ones were the losers in life's struggle. They were fit only to be controlled by European and American power. By spreading their superior culture around the world, the Anglo-Saxons would uplift the backward peoples.

It was a new version of the old cry of manifest destiny used to justify the war against Mexico in the 1840s. Now it fueled the program of commercial, military, and territorial expansion that was expected to bring America power and prosperity. Greed, self-ishness, self-pride, and hatred of others had shaped the cruel injustice to Indians, blacks, Asians, and the newer immigrants to America. Now they were shaping an attempt to master the world.

It was in these years that radical pacifism was rein-vigorated by teachings from abroad. The ideas of the Russian literary giant Leo Tolstoy (1828–1910) reached America through pamphlets, articles, and books. Here was an example of how ideas can arise in one place, move to another part of the world, and return to the place of origin. Converted to the gospel of peace in middle age, Tolstoy had corre-sponded years before with Adin Ballou, one of Garri-son's band of pacifists. The Russian had translated Ballou's writings and spread them in Russia. Now Tolstoy's own writings on nonresistance began to circulate in English in the United States, and several Tolstoy clubs sprang up to promote his ideas.

Tolstoy put his faith in Christian anarchism. He believed in the inviolable sanctity of human life, and that any use of force or violence was contrary to human dignity. Violence must be replaced by the law of Christian love, he held. He saw the state and property owners as the main source of everyday

Influenced by Thoreau's and Garrison's ideas, the Russian novelist Leo Tolstoy advocated resistance to any use of force or violence. His pacifist writings circulated widely in America.

evil. He urged the individual to resist nonviolently the state's illegitimate power and to take up the life of love and cooperation.

Tolstoy's ideas attracted many prominent Americans. The reformer Jane Addams, the lawyer Clarence Darrow, the Democratic Party leader William Jennings Bryan were strongly influenced by Tolstoy's faith in the ethic of nonviolence. They all tried to convert his ideas into practical programs.

A test for pacifist convictions soon came in the Spanish-American War of 1898. In Spain's island colony of Cuba, insurgents had long been fighting a war of national liberation. Their resistance to the brutal Spanish imperial regime had won the sympathy of many Americans. Supporters of the Cuban cause had mixed motives, however. Some hoped the Caribbean nation would gain an American-style freedom. Politicians in both parties wished to exploit the popularity of the Cuban cause for partisan ends. Businessmen wanted American annexation of Cuba to protect their investments on the island. Humanitarians wished for an end to the suffering and violence of the war.

Washington began to make proposals to Spain for solving the crisis that would bring the United States economic and strategic gains. In doing this, however, President McKinley did not consider the national aspirations and the economic well-being of the Cuban people. His was the arrogant view that Uncle Sam knew what was best for both Spain and Cuba. And he threatened military intervention if his proposals were not accepted.

In the first months of 1898, as the crisis mounted, McKinley sent the battleship *Maine* to Havana to protect, he said, American life and property. Seven days later the ship was destroyed by an explosion in the harbor that cost 260 lives. Whipped up by a war-hungry press, the American public demanded vengeance for the *Maine.* When Spain turned down another set of McKinley's proposals to solve the crisis on American terms, Congress declared war.

"A splendid little war," one American diplomat called it; it was swiftly over. Spain gave up Cuba and America occupied the island. The "Rising American Empire" also got from Spain the Caribbean island of Puerto Rico, and in the Pacific the island of Guam and all of the Philippines. The victory of Admiral Dewey over Spain at Manila brought the annexation of Hawaii. The United States now had a "legal" empire in the Pacific as well as a growing political and economic stranglehold over Cuba and Puerto Rico.

So many volunteers asked to serve in Cuba that the army took a hundred thousand more men than it could equip. There was no need for conscription. McKinley's crusade found the pacifists uncommonly quiet. The small UPU protested the war, and so did the APS. But it was all over so fast that the peace movement failed to rally many against the war.

What did come out of the war was a broad anti-imperialist movement. As rumors spread that the Administration planned to take over the Philippines, Boston reformers organized the Anti-Imperialist League to prevent the war from being "perverted into a war of conquest." A remarkable variety of leaders prominent in many fields supported the league—industrialists, journalists, feminists, educators, lawyers, urban reformers, blacks, trade unionists. They organized public meetings, mobilized supporters, and wrote articles, pamphlets, and books to make a strong case against McKinley's decision to seize the Philippines as a base to expand American power into Asia. They put forth many and sometimes conflicting arguments against American involvement in imperialist politics. But the heart of their opposition was the belief that imperialism was just plain wrong. It would corrupt our constitutional principles and cripple our democratic freedoms.

The league brought tremendous pressure on Capitol Hill against the treaty that would seize the Philippines. But the Senate ratified it by the margin of one vote needed to make the required two-thirds majority. Two days later, fighting broke out in the Philippines between American troops and Filipino patriots led by Emilio Aguinaldo.

The war for Philippine independence turned the Anti-Imperialist League into a mass movement. Membership shot up to thirty thousand, making the League the biggest antiwar organization (proportionate to population) in American history up to that time. Republicans, Democrats, independents, radicals joined labor, farm, and black leaders to broaden the movement beyond class and racial lines. Their goals were two: to stop the fighting in the Philippines and to get from Congress a pledge of Philippine independence. They wisely set aside all differences on other issues that might divide them in order to concentrate on the one question that united them.

But no amount of organization and agitation succeeded in stopping the war. Gradually U.S. military power ground down the insurrection, and McKinley won reelection in 1900, a bad blow to the anti-imperialist movement. The cost of the war was heavy. The Philippine people lost in battle some 20,000 men, and another 200,000 people died from famine and disease linked to the war. It took the United States forty-one months, over 4,000 lives, more than 2,800 wounded, and an outlay of $40 million to crush the guerrillas.

With the war's official end in 1902, the anti-imperialist movement dwindled to a northeast membership. Its leaders saw the growing power of the monopolies eager for foreign markets as a great danger to peace and democracy. They blamed white racism for justifying the suppression of the Filipinos. When reports of American atrocities in the Philippines reached home, the anti-imperialist movement forced a Congressional investigation of alleged war crimes in the islands. Commenting on its findings, the historian Charles De Benedetti wrote:

Fighting an irregular war against a colored people, U.S. armed forces had habitually tortured rebel suspects, shot prisoners or unlucky civilians, and burned and looted conquered areas. Yet there was little negative reaction within the country to the official confirmation of U.S. atrocities. Several dismissed the victims as "only niggers." Most editorialists excused U.S. military conduct as consistent with the irregular nature of the war, while leaders of organized Protestantism showed more concern with the Army's plans for licensed brothels in Manila than with war crimes. Perversely, the very power of national pride that anti-imperialists had hoped would shame Americans, once aware of the atrocities, into opposing the war, moved most people into accepting the crimes as the accidental but acceptable cost of a liberating war.

When Filipino resistance ended, the League continued its anti-imperialist work. Until 1920 it kept attacking American interference in Latin America as well as colonialism anywhere. Although popular support fell off badly, the League stubbornly carried on.

Mark Twain (1835–1910) was one of the country's noted literary figures who backed the League's attempt to rouse the country against America's inhuman warfare in the Philippines. Twain published in a national magazine a savage condemnation of General Funston's capture of Aguinaldo, the Filipino resistance leader, by a trick. Funston, home from the war to be hailed as a hero, advised such critics as Twain to be silent or risk being labeled traitor. Twain argued that Funston couldn't be blamed for his unsavory conduct "because his conscience leaked out through one of his pores when he was little."

On New Year's eve 1900 Twain sent out to the world this message:

A salutation speech from the Nineteenth Century to the Twentieth, taken down in shorthand by Mark Twain:

"I bring you the stately matron named Christendom, returning, bedraggled, besmirched, and dishonored, from pirate raids in Kia-Chou, Manchuria, South Africa, and the Philippines, with her soul full of meanness, her pocket full of boodle, and

her mouth full of pious hypocrisies. Give her soap and towel, but hide the looking-glass.''

It was his scorching comment on what he saw going on in the far corners of the world, where the Africans, the Filipinos, and the Chinese were receiving the blessing of Christianity and the bounty of civilization. In another article, in 1901, Twain attacked the imperialism of all nations. It brought him both furious condemnation and high praise. The response showed, he said, that "the nation is divided, half-patriots and half-traitors, and no man can tell which is which."

The question "which is which" bothered the leaders of the peace movement. They gave only partial support to the anti-imperialist crusade because they couldn't agree on what American imperialism was. Some backed McKinley's policies. Others opposed any move toward conquest. Too many of them were so optimistic about pacifism in the long run that they failed to resist Washington's aggression in the short run. And still others believed "our little brown brothers" abroad would only benefit from Christian disciplining.

Even the more progressive thinkers could give in to the temptation to swallow Washington's propaganda. What could be less selfish? the Administration asked: We are fighting for the noblest and most humane purpose—to free Cuba from the Spanish yoke. The woman's rights advocate Elizabeth Cady Stanton wrote, "Though I hate war per se, I am glad that it has come in this instance. I would like to see Spain . . . swept from the face of the earth."

To European pacifists, the Spanish-American War came as a profound shock. They had accepted America's self-evaluation as a righteous nation always on the side of the angels. Yet here was the United States traveling the same dirty path of empire as the much older nations of Europe. The war robbed them of one of their ready arguments for pacifism: that the United States was the example of a society that could live in peace because it had no evil designs on any other nation.

CHAPTER TEN

The War to End All Wars

The twentieth would be a century of great wars that would make America's war with Spain appear like a skirmish. Yet American pacifists entered the new century with an unbroken faith in their ability to spread peace at home and abroad. Nearly fifty new peace organizations appeared between 1901 and 1914. Their leaders came from the business and professional classes—lawyers, educators, clergymen, and corporation executives who desired an orderly world in which to expand their operations. The blessings of the businessmen made the peace cause a fashionable calling.

Most of the peace reformers supported U.S. leadership of the Western hemisphere and paid little attention to the colonial world. Their chief fear was that tensions in Europe would erupt in war. So they backed efforts to create stronger peacekeeping machinery and pressed Washington to take the lead in developing it.

Industrialists like Andrew Carnegie and lawyers like Elihu Root dominated the peace movement in the early 1900s. Their careers had made them believe you could take any problem to the courts. They pushed for an international tribunal whose impartial judicial decisions would settle disputes. With their great stake in the going socioeconomic system, the Carnegies and Roots wanted to defend property rights and Anglo-Saxon political power. To them it made good sense to hold prominent positions in the peace societies and just-as-prominent positions in the military-preparedness organizations. They were sure that peace meant law and order, and just as sure that law and order would be kept only by increasing Anglo-American might.

Their biggest success came in 1907, when they brought twelve hundred delegates of top government and private rank from eighteen nations to a peace congress in New York. Millionaires paid the bills, and over forty thousand people came to the seven sessions in Carnegie Hall. In size and respectability, no peace rally surpassed it. The spirit reached into the colleges, where campus peace groups took hold. In Boston, Fanny Fern Andrews formed the American School Peace League to spread international understanding to children. The old American Peace Society took on new life and organized nationally for the first time.

To meet demands for a more efficient and effective peace movement, two new organizations were formed. The World Peace Foundation acted through research and education to develop and distribute peace information, while the Carnegie Endowment for International Peace sponsored studies of the cause and cure of war.

A shift in the direction of the pacifist movement is clear in these early 1900s. Before, the peace advocates had had highly personal views of a world without war. Peace would come from living up to Christ's teaching; if every one of us did that, there would be no more war. After 1900, the stress fell more on creating international institutions to prevent war. The idealists who clung to the personal principles of Garrison, Tolstoy, and the Christian pacifists lost ground to the newcomers.

The new peace advocates became an elite. They had little contact with the mass of Americans. They did not grasp the lesson of the Spanish-American War—the menace of their nation's intervention in the affairs of weaker foreign states. Few of them criticized the armaments makers or dug deeply into the rivalries that fostered the arms race. And all too many could still be fired by the desire to impose America's ideas of peace, freedom, and justice upon the rest of the world.

The outbreak of world war in August 1914 testified to the failure of prewar peace efforts. Ten million soldiers were to die as the continent of Europe was devastated.

It seemed nobody wanted the war, yet nobody could stop it. Europe stumbled into a disaster that most men had not intended. The continent's major powers were linked by formal alliances that obliged them to go to war under certain conditions. Old rivalries between nations had threatened the peace for many decades. Disputes over colonies in Asia, Africa, and the Middle East could flare into war at any time. Germany and Austria-Hungary were bound in one alliance and Russia and France in a rival one. If something happened that led one power to declare war on another, then each power's allies were expected to join the fight against the other's allies. Given a quarrel between any two nations, all Europe could go up in flames.

By 1914 the unbearable tension had led to the stacking of huge armaments on all sides. Several times in the early 1900s friction had almost touched off a continental explosion. Each such crisis was blazoned in headlines across the world, adding to bitterness, hatred, and fear. Everyone feared war, dreading that some unexpected incident might set the juggernaut in motion.

It happened on June 28, 1914, when a young Serbian terrorist murdered the Austrian Archduke Franz Ferdinand at Sarajevo. This set Austria marching on Serbia. To protect Serbia, the tsar called 3 million Russians to arms, and France joined Russia in declaring war on Germany. When the kaiser's troops began to invade Belgium on the way to conquering Paris, England then joined France and Russia in the war.

The shot fired in a remote Balkan town had set off a chain of explosions that shattered peace worldwide. War had haunted Europe as far back as anyone could remember, but many people had convinced themselves that civilization had reached the point where disputes could be settled without resort to violence. There was great disappointment when the guns fired. Many Americans believed that the United States could and should stay out of the conflict in Europe. Some said the war could be of no benefit to America; others, that the Europeans had brought it on themselves and couldn't expect the United States to help them out of it.

News of the war's outbreak horrified America. *The New York Times* called it "the least justified of all wars since man emerged from barbarism" and said it was proof that European civilization was "half a sham." Ministers led prayers for peace and lamented what a miserable world this was to live in when nineteen hundred years after the birth of Christ we were on the brink of "the most disastrous and awful conflict in the world's history."

As soon as the war began, President Woodrow Wilson informed the leaders of the warring nations that he stood ready to help them restore peace. Parents gave thanks that their children were safely distant from the continent where English, French, German, and Russian boys were beginning to march on each other in a fury of blood. The exceptions were the Americans of foreign origin—French, German, Russian immigrants—whose natural sympathies lay with their homelands. But for most Americans, those Old World bonds had loosened. And the President, hoping to avoid commitment to one side or the other, publicly declared that "the United States must be neutral in fact as well as in name during these days that are to try men's souls." He appealed to the citizens to be "impartial in thought as well as in action."

But already some newspapers were blaming Germany for the war. She and Austria-Hungary had been the first to declare it, they said, and their armies had been the first to invade foreign soil. Stories of German atrocities in Belgium—some true, many false—spread rapidly. By 1915 the United States was still a neutral, but sympathy had swung strongly in favor of the Allies. That feeling, as well as the opportunity for profit, prevailed against Wilson's desire that American banks make no loans to any foreign nation at war. Wilson soon changed his policy, and huge sums were lent to France and Britain. American investors bought $2.3 billion in bonds from the Allies but only about $20 million in German bonds. U.S. trade with the Allies shot high, while exports to Germany and Austria dropped to almost nothing.

For a while the peace seekers, frustrated and resigned to the terrible fact of war, did nothing to try to stop it, but by 1915 some were ready to take part in a campaign against U.S. preparations for war. The movement was led by a group of progressive clergymen, social workers, and feminists. The new coalition saw war as the product of militarism and an imperialism that refused freedom to the nations under its heel.

An organization, the League to Enforce Peace (LEP), arose that brought together veterans of the old peace movement and newcomers. They talked of the need for a league of nations that would require its members to submit their disputes to a judicial council. But they advanced beyond this familiar idea to demand that league members "jointly use their military forces to prevent any one of their number from going to war" before submitting its dispute to some form of settlement. To keep the peace, they were asking for a collective threat of overwhelming retaliation against any warmaking nation. Well financed and staffed, the LEP rallied popular support for its ideas about collective security.

Pacifists and social workers such as Jane Addams and Lillian Wald organized nationally to press for neutral mediation in the war and to oppose American preparedness for entering it. The "real enemy," they said, is "militarism." The Woman's Peace Party was formed in Washington by three thousand prominent women to mobilize women internationally against war. They sent delegates to the International Congress of Women at The Hague in the spring of 1915. There the women agreed to call for a peace built upon national self-determination, international organization, and democratic control of foreign policy. Later that year the industrialist Henry Ford chartered a peace ship to carry neutral citizen-mediators to Europe. Their mission was to lobby the warring na-

The social reformer Jane Addams worked to carry out Tolstoy's belief in nonviolent resistance to war. She proposed international mediation to halt World War I, and when the United States entered the conflict, she held out against it. She led the Women's International League for Peace and Freedom for many years, and earned the Nobel Peace Prize in 1931.

tions to stop fighting and settle their disputes on the principles of justice and humanity. But they were only laughed at or ignored. The dying went on.

Sickened by the continuing carnage, a group of ministers, Quakers, and YMCA officials met in New York that fall to seek a solution to the suffering. They formed the Fellowship of Reconciliation (FOR), committed to Christian pacifism and a refusal to sanction war in any form. The young minister Norman Thomas joined FOR, declaring he had finally become convinced that "war and Christianity are incompatible; that you cannot conquer war by war; cast Satan out by Satan; or do the enormous evil of war that good may come." The Fellowship became the vehicle for all those who wanted to make pacifism an active instrument of reform.

That same year, some thirty-five hundred young men enrolled in the new Anti-Enlistment League. They signed this pledge:

I, being over 18 years of age, hereby pledge myself against enlistment as a volunteer for any military or naval service in international war, either offensive or defensive, and against giving my approval to such enlistment on the part of others.

In these months Wilson was shifting to a policy of getting the country prepared for war. He asked

Congress for a bigger military budget, for a 400,000-man army, and for new fighting ships. His proposals sparked a bitter public debate. Liberals created the American Union Against Militarism (AUAM) to oppose Wilson's military requests. It raised funds, built local chapters, campaigned against plans for conscription, distributed literature, and toured speakers to rallies across the country. But it failed to halt the government's rearmament program. In May 1916 Congress gave Wilson almost all he had asked for.

While the liberals were against the President's preparedness plans, they were for his progressive social legislation. So when he ran for reelection that fall, they backed him. Jane Addams, the philosopher John Dewey, and socialists John Reed and Scott Nearing were typical of many who voted for Wilson. Observers agree that Wilson owed his victory to the slogan of the Democrats—"He Kept Us Out of War."

Soon after the election, Wilson called for "a peace between equals." But two weeks later he broke diplomatic relations with Germany when it announced its submarines would attack any ship (including American) bound for Britain or France. Peace advocates pleaded for restraint and a popular referendum on any decision for war. Their cry went unheard.

On April 2, 1917, the new Congress met to hear Wilson's address. It was a war message. He condemned the German submarine policy as "warfare against mankind" and asked Congress to declare war. He called for the conscription of young men, the first federal draft since the Civil War. He demanded the enforced loyalty of all Americans in a cause that had split the country profoundly. And he insisted on heavy taxes and the enormous expansion of presidential power to meet the emergency. "The world must be made safe for democracy," he said.

The debate over the war resolution showed how deep was the split between prowar and antiwar forces. The former saw the war as a contest between democracy and autocracy, with the United States bound to line up on the side of right. The latter called it hypocrisy to demand war in the name of democracy. Senator George W. Norris of Nebraska spoke for them: "We are going into war upon the command of gold . . . I feel that we are about to put the dollar sign on the American flag." Like Norris, Senator Robert LaFollette of Wisconsin charged the war would only benefit the rich and harm the great mass of Americans. Shouts of "Treason! Treason!" greeted both their speeches on the Senate floor. But the two men voiced a widely popular feeling.

The same antiwar forces argued against compulsory military service. If public opinion is supposed to rule in a democracy, they said, then "a cause for

Jeannette Rankin of Montana, the first woman elected to Congress, in her maiden speech pleaded for the United States to stay out of the First World War. A pacifist from then on, she campaigned for over fifty years against U.S. involvement in all wars.

war should be so plain and so just and so necessary that the people would rise as one man to volunteer their lives to support the cause." But was this the case now? No—to raise and arm troops, the United

States had to adopt the same German-style militarism and conscription that it had denounced.

On the House floor on April 6, Representative Jeannette Rankin of Montana, the first woman elected to the U.S. Congress, made her maiden speech as she answered the roll for the vote on war: "I want to stand by my country, but I cannot vote for war. I vote no." (With that single act she became publicly identified as a pacifist for the first time. From then until her death fifty-six years later she campaigned against U.S. involvement in all wars.) Six senators and fifty representatives finally voted against war. But the majority decided for it, and in we went.

CHAPTER ELEVEN

We Are So Few Now

When the United States declared war, it had only 200,000 men in uniform. Before it ended, nearly 5 million Americans would serve in the armed forces. Of these, 2.8 million were to be drafted. In May 1917 Congress considered the first conscription bill since the Civil War, requiring all males between eighteen and thirty-five to register for the draft.

Critics in Congress called a draft un-American and said big business and high finance wanted a huge army and navy for conquest abroad and to put down dissension at home. Outside Congress, so many opposed conscription that President Wilson feared the bill might lose. He pleaded that the safety of the nation depended on it, and with strong pressure from the press and the pulpit, the draft went through.

Within weeks men who had opposed the draft were arrested and convicted on charges of seditious conspiracy. They were fined as much as $10,000 and given a year or more in federal prison.

Ten million young Americans were ordered to register locally on June 5 and take green draft cards with numbers on them. Resistance had been expected, but perhaps because of the arrests already made and highly publicized, there was little of it. In Racine, Wisconsin, when a young tin worker said he would not register and fight, he was forced to crawl on his knees to the flag spread on the floor and after kissing it compelled to salute.

Registration Day showed the President that, now that we were in the war, the great mass of Americans would go along. But there was a minority—a small one—that refused to go along with the majority. They were the militant men and women who had openly opposed Wilson's getting into the war.

Wilson feared that if this minority kept speaking out, it would injure morale and induce others to defy the draft law, so he imitated the warring nations: They had all taken emergency measures against espionage and subversion. In June 1917 Wilson approved the Espionage Act, which gave the government the right to censor the press, ban publications from the mail, and imprison anyone who interfered with conscription or the enlistment of soldiers. It was a powerful means of silencing the antiwar opposition. If Wilson could not have loyalty freely given, he would compel it.

Few Americans sympathized with the war protesters. Most were ready to call them traitors and fling them into jail. But most of the people who would suffer under the new law had no ties with the German enemy; they were only men and women who resisted America's going to war because it was against their moral and political convictions. The penalties for violating the law were harsh—twenty years in prison and a $10,000 fine.

Many magazines and newspapers were suppressed by the government under the Espionage Act. It did not matter how light their criticism of any detail of the war effort. Thousands of people were jailed for talking or writing against the war, and far more were frightened into hiding their views. A Vermont minister got fifteen years in prison just for telling his Bible class that "a Christian can take no part in the war."

The President helped to spread the virus of fear. Even before the United States entered the war, Wilson had attacked "hyphenated Americans," accusing them of pouring "the poison of disloyalty into the very arteries of our national life. . . . Such creatures of passion, disloyalty and anarchy must be crushed out. . . . The hand of our power must close over them at once."

That violent prejudice, mixed with a phobia against radical ideas, sank deeper and deeper into the American mind. Before 1914 German-Americans had been highly praised as among our most worthy citizens. Now a mindless anger raged so high against them that people feared to speak German in any public place. In Missouri, while five hundred patriots cheered, a mob lynched young Robert Prager, a German-born citizen who had tried to enlist but had been rejected on medical grounds. At the trial of the mob's leaders, their defense lawyer called their deed "patriotic murder" and the jury quickly declared them not guilty.

Some of those persecuted by the government stood out above the anonymous thousands who were made to suffer for sharing the same antiwar views. One of these was Emma Goldman, the salty, gray-haired anarchist who had had the courage to call President Wilson a hypocrite for denying freedom of speech and thought during a war "to make the world safe for democracy." When her Non-Conscription League held meetings to protest militarization of the nation, she was arrested, tried, and sentenced to two years in prison and fined $10,000.

In Chicago, the government put on trial for sabotage and conspiracy to obstruct the war 101 members of the Industrial Workers of the World (IWW), nicknamed the Wobblies. Lumberjacks, miners, harvest hands, editors, they were victims of the wartime hysteria and had no chance of getting a fair trial. In the end, 15 of their leaders were sentenced to twenty years in jail with fines of $30,000; 33 others got ten years, and the rest shorter sentences. They took their heavy blow with courage. One defendant told the judge: "The day that I leave jail I shall recommence those activities in behalf of humanity and the working class for which you are sentencing me today."

The Socialist Party became the special target of official wrath. In 1916, Eugene V. Debs (1855–1926), its presidential candidate, had polled 600,000 votes. The party now branded Wilson's call for war "a crime against the people" and urged "vigorous resistance" to the draft. Swiftly the government banned from the mails hundreds of Socialist publications and attacked the party leadership. Several of the most prominent Socialists caved in and switched to support of the war. They were like the European socialists, the majority of whom, in a nationalist fever, had lined up behind their governments when war broke out. They were all theoretically opposed to wars, holding them to be fought only for the benefit of the ruling classes. They had dreamed of calling an international general strike the day war was declared, a strike that would rob the generals of their troops and the munitions plants of their workers. But they fell easy victims to each of their governments' claims to be fighting a just battle for freedom, and shouldered rifles obediently to defend the fatherland.

Much of the American Socialist leadership was sent to prison. Kate Richards O'Hare got five years for an antiwar speech, and Rose Pastor Stokes got ten years for writing an antiwar letter to a newspaper. Debs, the popular head of the party, went on a speaking tour to defy the government's ban on antiwar speech. In Canton, Ohio, he told a cheering audience of workers,

The master class has always declared the wars; the subject class has always fought the battles. The master class has had all to gain and nothing to lose; the subject class has nothing to gain and all to lose—especially their lives.

Two weeks later Debs was arrested for this speech, found guilty, and sentenced to ten years in prison. In 1920, while in Atlanta penitentiary, he ran for President and received nearly 1 million votes.

The nation's schools became seeding grounds to

prepare young minds for war. In the elementary schools, "Patriotism, Heroism, and Sacrifice" were made the themes of "war study courses" engineered by both governmental and private propaganda agencies. War was presented as a "glamorous adventure" filled with heroic deeds. The struggle between tyranny and democracy was dramatized, with Germany in one role and the Allies in the other. Any discussion of other causes for war, such as nationalism or imperialism, was forbidden. Germany alone had caused the war, her soldiers alone behaved brutally, and only the Allies wanted peace. It was a grossly oversimplified black-and-white approach designed to stifle independent thought, not encourage it. The government mobilized the high schools and colleges, too, using stereotypes and hate propaganda to whip the young men into shape for military service.

In many schools throughout the country, the teaching of German, the "barbarian tongue," was stopped. Teachers of German were called traitors. German textbooks were publicly burned. People with German names were beaten by mobs. Hymns, symphonies, and operas of German origin were no longer played or sung. German-American cultural and sports clubs were disbanded. Many with German-sounding names hurried to change them.

Some men refused to register for the draft in order

to test the law in court. When the issue came before the U.S. Supreme Court in 1918, that body ruled unanimously that authority for the draft was found in Article I, Section 8 of the Constitution. It gave Congress the right to declare war and to raise and support armies.

As we saw with earlier wars, the burden of the draft fell unequally on the public. The poor and the powerless got far fewer exemptions than the prosperous and the highly placed. Physical condition, family hardship, and occupation were considered, and registrants were judged for their value to the war effort at home. Unskilled and blue-collar workers would contribute least, they were told, so they were drafted first. One Georgia draft board exempted 526 of 815 whites but only 2 of 202 blacks. Students got favored treatment. The Student Army Training Corps allowed 145,000 men to drill while they continued their studies. By the time their schooling was over, so was the war. Unlike that of the Civil War, this draft made no allowance for substitutes or commutation fees.

In this war, too, many men resisted military service for reasons of conscience. The draft law exempted members "of any well-recognized religious sect or organization . . . whose existing creed or principles forbid its members to participate in war in any form." But such COs, unlike other exempted groups, had to perform "in any capacity that the President shall declare to be non-combatant." The law recognized the traditional peace churches—Quakers, Mennonites, Church of the Brethren, Jehovah's Witnesses, and Hutterites.

The number of men applying for CO status rose from 1,500 in the Civil War to nearly 65,000 in World War I. Most were from the peace churches. Of these, 56,000 were accepted by the boards. About 21,000 of them got called to noncombat service, with 4,000 of them refusing at first to accept such duty. About 1,300 of this last group, under pressure, changed their minds and did accept it.

It was the absolutists again who refused to cooperate in any way. The military courts were severe with them. Death sentences were meted out to 17 of them (never carried out); 142 got life prison terms, and 345 got terms averaging some sixteen years. Only in 1933 did a presidential pardon from Franklin Roosevelt secure the release of the last of these men.

Treatment of the COs who chose the absolutist position varied from camp to camp. Cruelty in some of the camps was notorious. A congressional inquiry disclosed that guards had struck COs, fed them only on bread and water, placed them in solitary confinement, chained them to their cell bars, and hung them by their thumbs.

The letters sent by COs to friends and family, along with public hearings and press reports, brought their cause to the attention of sympathetic liberals. Organizations such as the National Civil Liberties Bureau (later to become the American Civil Liberties Union) defended their rights in the courts. The majority of the COs from peace sects were willing to accept alternate service, and these were not persecuted. It was the absolutists, and the nonreligious and political objectors, who aroused the fiercest hatred. They were labeled "slackers," "yellowbacks," "atheists," or "pro-Germans." To most Americans, being a pacifist meant being a coward, a radical, a foreigner who did not belong in America and had no rights the government need respect.

By this time, new waves of immigration had brought members of other peace churches into the country. These included Doukhobors, Molokans, Russellites, Christadelphians, Plymouth Brethren, and River Brethren. They, too, asked for exemption from military service, some as absolutists.

At Fort Leavenworth, six Molokans—Christian nonresisters from Russia—refused to work and were sent to the "hole," each one placed in a pitch-black cell, manacled standing to the bars for nine hours every day, then made to sleep on the bare cement floor. They endured this treatment for fifty-five days without giving in, before relief was permitted on orders from above.

Roderick Seidenberg, a young architect, was one of the COs placed in a stockade at Fort Leavenworth. He found himself with men from all quarters of the country and all walks of life. They were religious farmers from the Midwest, Wobblies from the Far West, socialists from New York's East Side, sailors, carpenters, college students, tailors. One was a statistician, another a prizefighter, another a music teacher, and all shared his convictions against war.

Seidenberg commented on how everything the COs believed in had been stood on its head by the government and most of the public:

We had refused to participate in organized slaughter; we were considered insensitive and unfeeling toward the higher causes of humanity. We had thought to stand aloof from the madness of war; we were antisocial and doctrinaire. We had taken what appeared to us the one direct and positive and unarguable position for peace; we were negative obstructionists. We had refrained from any propaganda, we believed in freedom of conscience; we were egocentric heretics. We thought ourselves tolerably sane; we were psychopathic.

For refusing to clean up the parade grounds, Seidenberg was sentenced to life at hard labor. But with the war over, he was released after eighteen months.

One of the many COs who tried to help the public understand why a CO took the position he did was Carl Haessler, a Rhodes Scholar at Oxford and a philosophy instructor at the University of Wisconsin. In a public statement he said:

America's participation in the World War was unnecessary, of doubtful benefit (if any) to the country and to humanity, and accomplished largely, though not exclusively, through the pressure of the Allied and American commercial imperialism.

Holding this conviction, I conceived my part as a citizen to be opposition to the war before it was declared, active efforts for a peace without victory after the declaration, and a determination so far as possible to do nothing in aid of the war while its character seemed to remain what I thought it was. I hoped in this way to help bring the war to an earlier close and to help make similar future wars less probable in this country.

I further believe that I shall be rendering the country a service by helping to set an example for other citizens to follow in the matter of fearlessly acting on unpopular convictions instead of forgetting them in time of stress. The crumbling of American radicalism under pressure in 1917 has only been equalled by that of the majority of German socialist leaders in August, 1914.

Haessler was what is called a "selective objector." He believed the war was an unjust one, fought for commercial and nationalistic reasons. He did not say he was opposed to *all* wars, only to this one. The courts—then and now—permit CO status only to "persons who oppose participating in all wars." Haessler was arguing that it was wrong to kill for *this* cause, at *this* time, under *these* conditions. He raised the claim of conscience against the will of the majority. And he was prepared to take the consequences.

Among the COs who took an absolutist position, but not on religious grounds, was Roger Baldwin. A Harvard graduate, his family among the first settlers of New England, he had opposed the draft as director of the American Union Against Militarism and then of its successor organization, the National Civil Liberties Bureau. Totally committed, he resigned his post and told his draft board that he would refuse induction. In 1918, twelve days before the armistice that would end the war, he was sentenced to a year in federal prison.

Standing before the court, Baldwin said:

The compelling motive for refusing to comply with the draft act is my uncompromising opposition to the principle of conscription of life by the State for any purpose whatever, in time of war or peace. I not only refuse to obey the present conscription law, but I would in future refuse to obey any similar statute

For refusing to be drafted in World War I, Roger Baldwin, like many other conscientious objectors, served a year in federal prison. He regarded conscription for any purpose, in peace or war, a violation of individual freedom, democratic liberty, and Christian teaching. Later he founded the American Civil Liberties Union.

which attempts to direct my choice of service and ideals. I regard the principle of conscription of life as a flat contradiction of all our cherished ideas of individual freedom, democratic liberty and Christian teaching. I am the more opposed to the present act because it is for the purpose of conducting war. I am opposed to this and all other wars. I do not believe in the use of physical force as a method of achieving any end, however good.

Baldwin was asked if he wouldn't use physical force to protect the life of any person under extreme emergency. He replied: "I don't think that is an argument that can be used in support of the wholesale organization of men to achieve political purposes in nationalistic or domestic wars. I see no relationship at all between the two."

The question asked Baldwin is almost always asked of every CO in this form: "What would you do if your wife or sister or someone else you loved was being raped?" A CO might reply that he would respond nonviolently.

But, in practice, if a struggle developed he might kill the attacker. A CO could know what he ought to do but couldn't know what he actually would do. Except that he certainly wouldn't gas the attacker or bombard him with artillery fire. Both common sense and the law agree that to defend yourself from a personal attack is not the same as making war. A soldier kills when he is ordered to, not just when he is attacked. That is what Baldwin meant when he said personal defense has nothing to do with being part of an army fighting a war.

Baldwin realized it was almost hopeless in time of war hysteria to get across the views of someone damned as a heretic. He knew his ideas were extremely unpopular. But, he said, "I fully believe that they are the views which are going to guide in the future."

In sentencing Baldwin, Judge Mayer gave the classic reply to the CO's position:

A Republic can last only so long as its laws are obeyed . . . [It] must cease to exist if disobedience to any law enacted by the orderly process laid down by the constitution is in the slightest degree permitted. . . . We should not be able to maintain what we regard as a Government of free people, if some individual, whether from good or bad motives, were able successfully to violate a statute . . . because his own view of the same might differ from that entertained by the lawmakers.

Roger Baldwin, in common with most COs, did not contest the judge's argument. A CO believes he must follow his own conscience and refuse to obey an unjust law. He stands willing to take the punishment for it in order to call public attention to the need to change that law.

Like Baldwin, Ernest Meyer was a nonreligious CO feared all the more by the government because he was not interested in his conscience alone. He wanted to get rid of a system that produced wars. Meyer was a student at the University of Wisconsin when the war began. His father, a German immigrant, had edited a socialist newspaper. At home young Meyer had absorbed the belief that behind most wars was greed for profits. What he learned about the origins of this war confirmed that idea. As editor of the campus paper, he wrote an article condemning the university for firing a professor who had joked about patriotism. He joined student rallies protesting the war and the draft. The university expelled him for his antiwar stand and the army drafted him.

Sent to a Kentucky camp, Meyer refused to put on the uniform and was called a "goddamn yellowback" by his sergeant. He was then put in a tent colony with other COs, isolated from the soldiers as though they were diseased. He was sent from camp to camp, each trying with abuse and humiliation and threat to bully him into submission. After many months of this he came close to asking for military duty. Then he remembered he was a CO not just to preserve his integrity. No, he was also testifying to his hope and belief that a time would come when war objectors would no longer be a "miserable handful" but

a clamoring host, so that word of our existence would travel on the wind to all corners, and men everywhere would spike

their guns and refuse longer to serve the warrior-imperialists
who have betrayed them. We are so few now. But later, in
the next war—for more will come, be sure of it—our ranks
may be formidable . . . our folded arms all-powerful.

When mobs savagely beat up opponents of war in the streets, it was no wonder that COs in the prisons were terrorized.

Evan Thomas led the protest against cruel treatment of prisoners at Leavenworth, the chief military prison. He had been sentenced to life imprisonment for his refusal to fight. He rejected conscription so thoroughly he would not eat or work under military authority, and was sent to Leavenworth. He went on a work strike, was put in the hole, chained to the bars, and forced to remain standing for eight to ten hours a day.

Other COs joined the protest against such harsh treatment and were sent to the hole, where they were not allowed to speak to one another. However, repelled by the brutality, the guards refused to enforce the nontalking rule. News of the strike leaked out. After seven weeks in solitary, Thomas and the others were released and the War Department made manacling illegal. It was by such common actions— work strikes and hunger strikes—that the COs sometimes forced the government to make reforms.

Perhaps the only people who refused publicly to register or serve and who got away with it were some tribes of Indians. In Arizona, the Navajos drove federal officers out of the reservation when they appeared to register the Indians for the draft. The government feared an Indian uprising if it persisted and made no further effort to register them. The Ute Indians of Colorado did the same thing.

There were the silent resisters, too—the draft evaders, as in every war. Estimates of the number who dodged the draft range from 170,000 to twice that number. Only 10,000 of them were prosecuted for failing to register.

When peace came it did not end the troubles of the opponents of war. President Wilson insisted they must pay the penalty for their "unpatriotic" behavior. A cry for amnesty went up, but few editors or religious leaders were willing to speak out for victims of the espionage and sedition acts.

The cost of this, the first of a chain of international wars, was beyond calculation. Two million Germans, 2 million Russians, 1 million French, 1 million English, 1 million Austrians and hundreds of thousands from other nations were shot, burned, bayoneted, gassed, bombed to death. Among them were the 30,000 American soldiers who died during the brief nineteen months America was in the war.

When the war began many saw it as a stage in human progress—"the war that will end war." But in the four years of fighting such acts of horror were committed by nations called civilized that mankind seemed headed for destruction.

In 1984 the scientist Freeman Dyson wrote about "the gravest problem now facing mankind, the problem of nuclear weapons." Looking back to the First World War he saw a lesson for today:

The First World War, taken as a whole, is a gigantic parable of the war that mankind is trying to avoid. It was a war of peculiar ugliness, fought with exceptional stupidity and brutality. It destroyed permanently a great part of European civilization. It was started for reasons that in retrospect seem almost trivial. The damage and loss suffered by all parties were utterly out of proportion to the pettiness of the initial quarrel between Serbia and Austria-Hungary. In all these respects, the history of the First World War holds up a mirror to the present, showing how small follies lead to great disasters, how ordinarily intelligent people walk open-eyed into Hell.

CHAPTER TWELVE

Is Pacifism Enough?

The young generation of Europe had gone eagerly to the front when World War I began. In its first months it was probably the most popular war in history. One Frenchman called the war "a marvelous surprise," and another reported that he "loved life at the front." A German writer said the fighting gave him "a new zest for life." The English poet Rupert Brooke found it "the only life—a fine thrill, like nothing else in the world." And to an Italian poet it was "the hour of the triumph of the finest values."

As the killing mounted into the millions, the enthusiasm turned into disgust and rage. The soldiers in the trenches on both sides promised themselves revenge upon the old men, the "guilty politicians" who had ruined their world and destroyed their future. But this was not felt at first by the Americans, who saw action late and only briefly. It took longer for their high tide of idealism to recede, but by the early 1920s the veterans were writing novels voicing the bitter disillusionment that had set in. Readers turned to John Dos Passos, Thomas Boyd, William Faulkner, E. E. Cummings, and William March to discover a literature of protest against the war, dispelling any illusions about its adventure, its romance, its idealism. Ernest Hemingway, who had been in the ambulance service at the front, published his *A Farewell to Arms*. In it occurs the famous passage where the hero thinks:

I was always embarrassed by the words sacred, glorious, and sacrifice and the expression in vain. We had heard them, sometimes standing in the rain almost out of earshot, so that only the shouted words came through, and had read them, on proclamations that were slapped up by billposters over other proclamations, now for a long time, and I had seen nothing sacred, and the things that were glorious had no glory and the sacrifices were like the stockyards at Chicago if nothing was done with the meat except to bury it. There were many words that you could not stand to hear and finally only the names of places had dignity. . . . Abstract words such as glory, honor, courage, or hallow were obscene beside the concrete names of villages, the numbers of roads, the names of rivers, the numbers of regiments and the dates. . . .

Apart from the horror of modern war itself was the failure of the hopes for a better world with which many Americans had entered it. The peace terms laid out by the victors in the Treaty of Versailles were harsh and punitive. President Wilson had wanted a negotiated compromise based upon justice and the right of all nations to self-determination. But he gave in to Georges Clemenceau and David Lloyd George, his French and British allies. They dictated terms that would reward the victors and punish the vanquished. The outcome was a formula for economic disaster and future war.

The Versailles Treaty provided for an organization, the League of Nations, to establish the machinery for a durable international peace. (The United States never joined the league.) But through the twenties and thirties it became clear that major powers would not go to war to enforce the League's decisions. Not unless their own vital interests were at stake. A universal system to which all powers belonged could not for this reason guarantee everyone's frontiers. (The same crucial fault would cripple the United Nations after World War II.)

World War I woke pacifists from the dream of inevitable progress toward peace. In the next decades peace seekers operated on many levels. They protested the spreading influence of militarism in American life. They promoted disarmament and peace education. They saw that simply being against the use of violence was not enough; they had to work for a society whose structure allowed no place for violence.

Pacifists of varying opinions sometimes combined forces in a common effort and at other times quarreled with each other. They could not agree on whether America should join the League of Nations, or later over how to resist German and Japanese expansion in the 1930s. One conviction, however, was common to them all. Before World War I they had believed peace was morally *right* and practically *desirable.* Now they knew that modern science and technology, rapidly accelerating and uncontrollable, had made peace *necessary* if mankind was to survive.

The postwar years saw the birth of several new peace groups. The movement appealed most strongly to professional women. Jane Addams, Emily Greene Balch, and others formed the Women's International League for Peace and Freedom (WILPF), based in Switzerland. Its focus was more on people than on governments. People had to eat before they could think about peace, so they organized national sections to direct nonviolent action against hunger and injustice.

For twelve years, up into the mid-thirties, the annual Conference on the Cause and Cure of War brought hundreds of delegates from large women's organizations to Washington. They debated peace issues and proposals and tried to build a strong women's coalition against war.

The War Resisters League (WRL), formed in 1923, took in anyone who pledged to renounce participation in war. Their hope was to stop the next war through a massive general strike. Much of the League's work was educational. It advocated conscientious objection and gave legal advice and support to those who needed it. Together with the Women's Peace Society, the Women's Peace Union, and the Fellowship of Reconciliation, they tried to open people's eyes to the folly of the First World War. They staged street demonstrations, with songs, candlelight ceremonies, and prayer services to draw attention to their cause. They supported congressional investigations into the causes of World War I. And when these exposed the role of the munitions makers and big business, they publicized the findings. Internationally they backed every step toward disarmament.

These moves culminated in 1929 in the Paris Peace

Pact. It outlawed war as a solution to international problems. Sadly, although sixty-two nations signed the pact, it did nothing to prevent them fighting each other in World War II.

In the 1930s college students joined women and the clergy as a major force in the peace movement. With many liberal and radical groups, they took part in a series of "No More War" parades. These started small but soon mustered as many as twenty thousand marchers. At Armistice Day services young men stepped forward to renounce war. When a student movement in England created the Oxford Pledge, thousands of young men in American universities, too, took the oath of absolute refusal to serve in the armed forces.

On a visit to America in 1931, the great German physicist Albert Einstein said that even if only 2 percent of those assigned to perform military service should announce their refusal to fight, governments would be powerless. He echoed the motto of the War Resisters League: "Wars will cease when men refuse to fight." In April 1935 sixty thousand college students went on a nationwide strike against war, and in November twenty thousand in New York alone paraded in the city streets against war.

It was in the Protestant churches that the peace movement made its greatest impact during the thir-

In the 1930s the antiwar movement spread to many college campuses. Students like these University of Chicago under-graduates joined with other pacifist groups in "No More War" parades, and thousands pledged absolute refusal to serve in the armed forces.

ties. The churches—except for the peace sects—had given almost unanimous support to the First World War. But now the Federal Council of Churches resolved that "the churches should condemn resort to the war-system as sin and should henceforth refuse . . . to sanction it or to be used as agencies in its support." Various denominations joined in peace actions. The pacifist position took firm hold not only among church leaders but in the student Christian movement, the seminaries, and the upper grades of the Sunday schools.

Jewish religious opinion, too, turned toward pacifism in the early thirties. Several national Jewish organizations affiliated with militant peace societies. Condemnation of war also increased among Catholics. The Catholic Worker movement, launched in New York by Peter Maurin and Dorothy Day in 1933, combined religious and radical concerns. Its newspaper, *The Catholic Worker*, carried many articles on the immorality of war and conscription. It rejected the idea of a "just war" as a contradiction in terms and asserted the Catholic's right to a CO position. The movement became the leading voice in American Catholic circles for militant pacifism.

Off on the left, communists, socialists, and liberals built a "united front" organization called the American League Against War and Fascism. Almost all but the communists eventually withdrew over policy disputes, but the League remained active through the thirties, holding many demonstrations against war.

American farmers gave some support to the peace movement, with three of their national groups endorsing it. But few of the trade unions, except for some left-wing ones, showed any interest.

A vigorous force for peace was the National Council for the Prevention of War (NCPW). Founded by Quaker pacifist Frederick J. Libby in 1921, to bring together peace-minded groups of all kinds, by the mid-thirties the NCPW had headquarters in Washington, where it lobbied Congress, and branch offices throughout the country. It coordinated the peace efforts of some thirty national organizations, distributing from 1 to 2 million pieces of literature annually and feeding press information and radio programs nationwide.

Peace groups warned against the dangers of America's powerful economic and political role overseas. When Washington sent troops into Nicaragua in 1926, the peace activists lobbied Congress for withdrawal of U.S. forces. They demanded that the Administration settle peaceably its persisting differences with Mexico, and they asked that it liberate America's Philippine colony.

From one group after another came warnings of threats to peace raised by America's new role in world affairs. The country, said one critic, "must decide whether it shall be an empire or a democracy." Another feared that "the vastness of America's foreign investments" might trap the country "unknowingly and unwillingly in the mazes of economic imperialism."

To counter pacifist and liberal views, conservative forces mustered their strength. The American Legion and the Ku Klux Klan called for greater military muscle to be put behind expansion abroad and attacked peace seekers as radicals and subversives. A War Department chief prepared a spiderweb chart to show links between peace, social welfare, and religious groups and claimed that they were all part of an international socialist plot.

Fascism itself appealed to many Americans during the depression years. A native variety of Hitlerism took hold. Henry Ford—the same Ford who financed a peace ship—had carried on a campaign against the Jews in the 1920s, and in 1938 he accepted a medal from Hitler. The Catholic priest Father Charles E. Coughlin roused millions of listeners with weekly radio speeches praising Hitler, Mussolini, and Franco as "patriots" rising to the challenge of communism. The popular fundamentalist preacher Gerald Winrod said that nazism and fascism stood for "life, happiness and prosperity." The newspaper publisher William Randolph Hearst visited Hitler in 1934 and reported he was "an extraordinary man" whose "great policy, great achievement" was to have saved Germany from communism. The German-American Bund paraded the streets in storm trooper uniforms and applauded Hitler's racism and militarism.

With the outbreak of the war, the fascist movement in the United States faded. The deep-rooted anti-Semitism it represented, however, was a powerful factor in preventing America from offering asylum to Hitler's Jewish victims.

Although none of the pacifist groups ever won mass membership, their activities did reach out to many millions of Americans who shared the pacifist impulse. In the early thirties, however, a profound shift in world politics began to make itself felt. The totalitarian regimes of Mussolini in Italy and Hitler in Germany and the militarists in Japan chalked up a series of conquests that forced a change in American opinion. One after another, independent nations—Spain, Albania, Austria, Czechoslovakia, Ethiopia, China—fell victim to fascism. That system valued war as both means and end. How would the peace movement respond to it?

By the mid-thirties it was clear that the League

of Nations would fail to arrest fascist aggression. The organized peace movement began to split apart. Some of its elements remained staunchly pacifist and tried to insulate America from the threat of war in Europe. Religious pacifists asked America to remain neutral "because war is futile" and "an evil thing contrary to the mind of Christ."

Americans who felt an ethical horror of war were the first to be horrified by the evils of fascism. Its destruction of personal liberty, its contempt for democracy, its glorification of war, its murderous anti-Semitism made some pacifists begin to think that a war against fascism represented the lesser of two evils. If all else failed, militarism must be met with militarism. It was a shift in position similar to the one among the Quaker and other pacifist abolitionists when they chose to take up arms against slavery.

Albert Einstein, an active pacifist since 1914, and in the thirties a fugitive from nazism, wrote that

the existence of two great powers with definitely aggressive tendencies (Germany and Japan) makes an immediate realization of movement toward disarmament impracticable. The friends of peace must concentrate their efforts rather on achieving an alliance of the military forces of the countries which have remained democratic.

Sherwood Eddy, a leader among religious pacifists,

gave up his faith in it. "Nothing could stop [fascist powers]," he said, "except the use of force." Reinhold Niebuhr, a pacifist clergyman who had chaired the Fellowship of Reconciliation, resigned from it and attacked pacifists who called for American neutrality at the time of Japanese aggression in Manchuria. He said, "We can justify the refusal to take such risks only if we believe that peace is always preferable to the exploitation of the weak by the strong."

The pacifists who remained committed to peace were not silent in the face of fascism. They were among the first to organize protests against Hitlerism and to try to open America's doors to its helpless victims. (But polls showed that not 8 percent of the American people were willing to admit Jewish refugees into the country.)

Nor did pacifists want to appease the fascist powers. They did not believe surrendering to every demand of the dictators would keep the peace. They detested what fascism stood for. But, they asked, was war a solution to the problem? If heavy rearmament for war by the democracies was supposed to halt fascism, then the "cure" resembled the disease, argued some pacifists. Henry J. Cadbury, chairman of the American Friends Service Committee, wrote:

Friends may sympathize with the alleged ends of a war;

they may recognize as fact the situation which seems to others to recommend war. But that war is the way to deal with this situation or to strive toward these ends does not automatically follow. If flagrant abuse of its own citizens or of other peoples is practised by a foreign power, violence on our part may involve other innocent persons and may not reduce the evil results.

CHAPTER THIRTEEN

A Terrible Moral Dilemma

As the world mobilized for war, a great many Americans believed the United States should stay out of it at all costs. Descend into the storm cellar, they said, and let the hurricane blow over us. The desire to isolate America from the clash of arms was so strong that Roosevelt could not get Congress to adopt even a modest program of collective security. The legislators feared such measures might drag the country into war. The Neutrality Act they did pass barred selling arms to both sides in any war.

Only after Hitler began World War II in 1939 by invading Poland and then Western Europe did a change of heart take place. FDR and the Congress took one step after another to make America "the arsenal of democracy." They increased aid to Britain and pumped huge funds and energy into speeding up American military production. "Your boys are not going to be sent into foreign wars," FDR promised. But in September 1940 Congress adopted the first peacetime program of compulsory military service in U.S. history. The next month all men between twenty-one and thirty-five (16.4 million) were registered for the draft and the training of the first million troops began.

In spite of the isolationists, the Administration gradually edged its way into the war. FDR presented the struggle against Hitler as a righteous cause and early in 1941 held up a vision of a new world order to be founded upon the "Four Freedoms"—freedom of speech and expression, freedom of worship, freedom from want, and freedom from fear. In August he met with the British war leader, Winston Churchill, aboard ship in the Atlantic; they affirmed that the broad aims of the two great powers would be peace and collective security for all nations. Soon fifteen other countries, including the Soviet Union (which Hitler had invaded in June), endorsed the Atlantic Charter.

On Sunday morning, December 7, Japanese naval and air forces launched a devastating attack on the U.S. naval base at Pearl Harbor in Hawaii. The next day, with only one dissenting vote—by Jeannette Rankin, who had voted against U.S. entry into World War I—the Congress declared war on Japan. Three days later, Germany and Italy supported their Axis partner by declaring war on the United States.

If any war could be called a "just" war, this seemed to many to be it. The overwhelming majority of Americans were not spoiling for a fight, but after Pearl Harbor 96 percent showed in a poll that they considered World War II a necessity. What else could you do against a power like Hitler's but resist it? For many pacifists it was a terrible moral dilemma. They had seen the threat of fascism long before most others, and had spoken up against it. As he watched some of his pacifist friends put aside their nonviolence and take up arms against Hitler, the absolutist Evan Thomas said he could understand why they did it. But, he asked, what would be the result? "Following the last war," he wrote,

I saw enough actual discrimination and brutality in this country to realize that people like Hitler were not unique. I had to make up my mind at that time what I considered to be the best form of resistance to that sort of thing. . . . I came to the conclusion . . . that violence is no answer to tyranny, exploitation or brutality.

But what if, as in Europe, your country was invaded by a nation like Hitler's? One pacifist, Jessie W. Hughan, wrote a pamphlet, "If We Should Be Invaded," describing how a people could nonviolently resist invasion even by a ruthless aggressor. The examples of nonviolent resistance by the Norwegians and Danes to Nazi occupation gave pacifists ground to believe that their method could be an effective social force against war and for making this a better world to live in.

The Germans invaded Norway in April 1940, taking the people completely by surprise. Norway held out longer against the blitzkrieg than any other European state—sixty-three days—but finally was overcome. The king and leadership sailed to London and set up a government in exile. The Norwegians at home gradually sank all party differences and worked out a pattern of nonviolent resistance to the Nazi occupation. The church in a pastoral letter ringingly denounced the lawlessness and brutality of the Brownshirts and attacked the destruction of human rights. Every section of the people refused cooperation with Nazi control: only four of three thousand athletic teams took part in contests; twelve thousand of fourteen thousand teachers refused to obey orders to nazify the children; workers resigned en masse from the nazified trade unions. People stopped reading the nazified press or going to Nazi movies. Over two hundred underground newspapers appeared, and an underground radio station spread the truth and the news to listeners secretly tuning in. When the Germans ordered up young men born in certain years for forced labor, the people evaded the call by losing or changing birth certificates, and by burning office records. The Nazis got only three hundred of the eighty thousand eligible men. Saboteurs wrecked trains and tracks to impede German movements and kept the British fully informed of German actions. The Germans captured, tortured, sent to concentration camps, or executed saboteurs or suspects, but the people's will to resist was never broken.

That same April month of 1940, the Germans attacked Denmark. With virtually no army, the government had to give up. Here, too, as in Norway, there were some Nazi sympathizers, but only a handful, not 3 percent of the popular vote. The Germans tried conciliation at first, to win the Danes' cooperation, but that failed. When resistance grew, the Germans blamed it on the Jews, though Denmark had less than seven thousand Jews. In October 1943 the Germans ordered the entire Jewish population to be rounded up. But word leaked out in advance, and overnight, by bicycle and car, by boat and raft and swimming, some six thousand of the intended victims were spirited out of the country to safety in Sweden. The Nazis captured about six hundred; most of them died in Buchenwald. The Germans intensified their brutality, but the Danes resisted by strike and sabotage. Denmark became a "peaceful battlefield," and when the German armies collapsed in May of 1945, the Danes were proud they had played a part in their own liberation.

The barrage of prowar propaganda was less heavy this time than in the First World War, and the use of censorship was milder. The treatment of conscientious objectors, too, was more humane. The pacifists, reading the signs correctly, knew they were in for another lonely defense of their convictions. Before the war began they started to build support for individual COs. The historic peace churches reaffirmed their commitment to nonresistance. In the mainline Protestant denominations, COs formed small fellowships. Guided by the Catholic Worker movement, the Association of Catholic COs was formed.

As soon as FDR moved toward massive military mobilization, the pacifists pressed for the recognition of a nonmilitary status for COs. Recall that CO status is not a constitutional right, only a privilege. The Administration finally agreed to classify as a CO any person "who, by reason of religious training and belief, is conscientiously opposed to participation in war in any form."

This was better than the traditional exemption only of members of the peace churches. But it did not meet the pacifists' request that the scruples of nonreligious objectors be recognized equally. Nor did it recognize selective COs who refused to fight in some wars if not in all.

It's worth noting that during this war the British draft law allowed selective objection. CO status was granted to Welshmen who didn't want to fight for Britain, to Italian residents who didn't want to fight their fellow countrymen, and even to people who were pro-German.

Draft boards had authority to direct men both into and away from military service. In the early years of the war, they could defer students and men in certain occupations—doctors, engineers, scientists—but as manpower needs mounted, these deferments were closed to most. (College enrollments fell to one-third of their prewar levels.) Unlike other draft exemptions, CO status required alternative service. The number of COs grew as the war progressed, both in degree and in kind. Certain COs were allowed to perform alternative service outside the military, in civilian public service camps (CPS). While still requiring religious ground for recognition as a

CO, men no longer needed to be members of a peace church. It was up to local draft boards to decide who filled the requirement of a CO, and whether the CO should serve in the military as a noncombatant or work in a CPS camp.

About fifty thousand COs were assigned to the armed forces and did noncombatant duty. Another twelve thousand entered the CPS. And six thousand absolutists (nearly three fourths of them Jehovah's Witnesses) went to prison rather than take part in any aspect of the draft process. They would not accept alternative service. They believed conscription itself was essential to modern warfare and so evil that it had to be resisted.

Who were the men who took the CO position? In numbers, they were but a tiny percentage of the 13 million Americans who served in the armed forces in World War II. Almost none came from the working class; few were black, Hispanic, or Indian. Most were middle-class and well educated. They were largely professionals—teachers, social workers, artists, writers, actors. Not businessmen, but idealists or radicals.

As for their religious backgrounds, the great majority of COs were Protestant. Precise figures are lacking, but perhaps 160 were Catholic and 150 Jewish. The historic peace churches again rejected war.

The Mennonites had the best record: three of every five of them of draft age became COs. On the other hand, three fourths of all Quakers drafted declined to claim CO status, despite the official antiwar position of their church. For most of them it was a conflict in values, as when earlier Quakers in the Civil War shed their pacifism to fight for the defeat of slavery. Now, in this war, Quakers decided they had to fight to overthrow fascism.

The Jewish Peace Fellowship was formed early in the war to offer counsel and assistance to Jewish COs. Its board came from rabbis of all denominations—Orthodox, Conservative, and Reform. About 150 Jews entered CPS camps or went to jail for refusing cooperation in any form with the military or the war effort.

Within their own community, it was hard going for them. Hitler's murderous attack on Jews made many feel that Jews who chose to be COs were traitors to their people. Jewish laymen on draft boards would usually deny the request of the Jewish CO. How could a Jew in his right mind be a CO? They feared, too, that Jewish COs would be marked disloyal and feed anti-Semitism. To prove Jews loyal, they felt Jews in even higher proportion than others must fight in this war.

More Catholics became aware of the possibility

of conscientious objection in this war. There had been only one recorded Catholic CO in the First World War. Now some 160 entered CPS camps, and more might have been in other categories of objection. The chancery offices in the United States issued only a bare one-sentence statement saying that a Catholic could be a CO. Draft boards were hostile to them; because they didn't think the Catholic Church stood for that position, they sent them to prison. Yet Catholic COs followed a peace tradition going back to the earliest days of the Christian Church. In recent centuries, however, that tradition had been identified with the Protestant peace churches. Many Catholics forgot the roster of their own canonized saints honoring many men who were martyred for their refusal to bear arms. Priests and pastors as well as laymen mistakenly believed in these years that no Catholic had a right to be a CO on religious grounds.

The first men to object to the new draft law were eight Protestant students at Union Theological Seminary. Although eligible for ministerial deferments, the students refused to register. Their joint statement said:

It is impossible for us to think of the conscription law without at the same time thinking of the whole war system, because it is clear to us that conscription is definitely a part of the institution of war. . . . We have also been led to our conclusion on the conscription law in the light of its totalitarian nature. . . . We believe, therefore, that by opposing the Selective Service Law, we will be striking at the heart of totalitarianism as well as war.

The students were sentenced to prison terms of one year and a day. (Some of them were reindicted after their release and forced to serve second terms.) On the day of sentencing, they told the court that rather than choose "the vicious instrument of war," it was

all the more urgent to build in this country and throughout the world a group trained in the techniques of nonviolent opposition to the encroachments of militarism and fascism. When we do build such a movement, we will have found the only weapon which can ever give an effective answer to foreign invasion. Thus in learning to fight American Hitlerism we will show an increasing group of war-disillusioned Americans how to resist foreign Hitlers as well.

A legendary figure in the record of this war's COs was Corbett Bishop. His policy was absolute non-cooperation with the draft. He served three separate prison terms during the war, going a total of 426

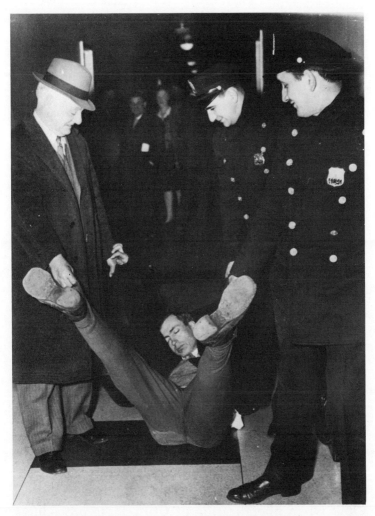

In World War II there were tens of thousands of conscientious objectors. Corbett Bishop, one of the most celebrated, is shown being carried by police because he refused to walk or move or take any action that meant cooperation with the draft.

days without taking food or water. After one arrest for walking out of a CPS camp because it was involuntary service, Bishop said, "The authorities have the power to seize my body; that is all they can do. My spirit will be free." He refused to walk, move, or take any action on his own part. He would not stir from his cot even to use the toilet. He made the prison officials fully responsible for his body. If they wanted him to move, they would have to carry him themselves. His resistance proved too much for them, and they released him unconditionally before his sentence was up. His nonviolent resistance was taken as a sign of what that method might achieve on a broader scale.

Many others walked out of CPS camps to protest the system as a form of conscription they wanted no part of. Two of these men, Stanley Murphy and George Taylor, were sentenced to two and a half years. Confined at Danbury Prison, they were immediately placed in solitary for refusing to work. They began a hunger strike to protest the imprisonment of COs; on the eighteenth day they were placed in hospital cells and force-fed through their noses. Only when liberalization of CO release procedures was promised did they end their fifty-four-day strike.

When nothing was done, Murphy and Taylor

threatened to resume their strike. Fearing they might die, the authorities quickly transferred them to a federal mental hospital. They were kept naked in a cell stripped of chairs and beds and beaten by the guards to force them to accommodate. They smuggled out letters documenting brutality and the fatal beating of a young black. Their exposé forced an investigation, which brought about prison reforms. Their militant example inspired many other COs in prisons and camps to protest through several techniques of nonviolent resistance.

Many other COs came to the attention of the press and public during World War II. Arlo Tatum, born of a Quaker family in Iowa, refused to register for the draft in 1940, when he turned eighteen, and was sentenced to three and a half years in prison. Nine years later, under the law of 1948, he was jailed for the same offense and served nearly eighteen months. His principled objection to war led him to work with COs in several executive posts—with the American Friends Service Committee, the War Resisters League, and the Central Committee for Conscientious Objectors. In 1943 Bayard Rustin, later a founder of the Congress of Racial Equality (CORE) and a leader of the civil rights movement, was imprisoned for three years as a CO.

The film actor Lew Ayres, who starred in the antiwar film *All Quiet on the Western Front*, was moved by that experience to become a CO. In 1942 he entered a CPS camp and later joined the medical corps. The film industry treated him like a traitor, refusing to show his movies, but 85 percent of the thousands of letters he got praised his decision. Several of the most prominent film actors, writers, and directors publicly backed his right to act on his own conscience.

The poet Robert Lowell, then a Catholic convert, was sentenced as a CO to a year and a day in Danbury Prison. Thomas Merton, later the Trappist monk who wrote *The Seven Storey Mountain*, was a CO while still a layman. David Dellinger, one of the Union Theological Seminary students sentenced, in 1940, to a year and a day for refusing to register, after his release refused assignment to a CPS camp and got a two-year sentence.

James Peck became a lifelong advocate of pacifism when, in 1933, at the age of eighteen, he read the German novel *All Quiet on the Western Front*, by Erich Maria Remarque. I saw, he said,

the futility of war through the eyes of a group of German soldiers in World War I. In the book, based on Remarque's own experiences, the Germans who had always been characterized to me as beasts were depicted as human beings. Like the boys on our side, they hated war but were forced to go to war and kill against their wills.

Throughout the thirties, Peck did what he could to influence people around him against war. His pacifism met a severe test with the Civil War in Spain. It seemed a just war when the Spanish democracy tried to defend itself against a fascist uprising aided by Hitler and Mussolini. Thousands of Americans volunteered to fight in the International Brigades, but Peck, somewhat shakily, stuck to his beliefs. In 1940, on the first day of registration for World War II, he declared himself a CO. He was jailed for over twenty-eight months for opposing the war. He thought that, as with the First World War, this one, too, had purely economic motives:

The real war aims of the Allies were to hold on to their respective empires for the purpose of exploiting them financially. The real war aims of the Axis nations were to appropriate these empires for themselves for the same purpose. The peoples of both sides had nothing to gain by slaughtering each other.

The Allies claimed the war was inevitable. Yet hadn't Britain and France armed Hitler as a bulwark against Russia? And hadn't the United States armed Japan for years, reaping a lucrative profit therefrom?

*   *   *

A novel experiment in the 1940 draft law regarding COs was the provision for the CPS camps. COs who refused noncombatant service under military authority had to perform work of "national importance" in the camps, which were sponsored by three traditional peace sects—Friends, Mennonites, and Brethren—and the Association of Catholic Conscientious Objectors. The CPS idea arose from two sources—the pacifist experience with voluntary work camps and the government's experience with the Civilian Conservation Corps during the 1930s depression. The CPS blended the two successes.

By May 1941 the first camps were set up under the Forestry Service, the Soil Conservation Service, and the National Park Service. Nearly twelve thousand COs would work for periods up to six years on such projects as soil erosion control, reforestation, or agricultural experimentation. As the armed forces drained off rural manpower, some COs were assigned to farms for replacement labor. Others took part in road building, health care, and social work. Some COs volunteered to be guinea pigs in medical experiments on malaria, hookworm, typhus, hepatitis, diet, or endurance.

Flaws in the CPS program soon became visible. Neither the COs in the camps nor their families received any compensation for their service. Those in church-run camps had to support themselves or be helped by their church or family. They got none of the benefits granted soldiers—compensation for injury or death, medical care, or allowance for dependents. During their service, their families were deprived of income.

That the CPS men received no pay was no accident. The government argued that if COs were free of risk, they should not be compensated. The draft authority hoped this would force some men to choose military duty. But, as some COs replied,

there was no more reason for treating them as criminals than for treating all the rest of the population outside the military in the same way. If it is suggested that young men are to be discouraged from claiming to be conscientious objectors . . . where is the authority in the Selective Service Act for doing so?

Sometimes the work done by the COs was dangerous to health, but worse, it was often meaningless, simply make-work to keep them busy. Soon the military moved in to take control of the camps, and under their powerful pressure the civilian direction was denied in spirit and practice. Upset by such developments, the social activists among the COs organized protests. It was easy to feel desperate: The pacifist movement was small and weak in the face of popular support for the war. And isolated in the camps and prisons, the COs felt all the more alone and forgotten. The protests fizzled out. Little was changed.

But the pacifist organizations and publications rallied to their support, reporting what was happening in the camps and prisons and demanding better treatment. Julius Eichel, himself an imprisoned CO in World War I, fought for the rights of COs in prison and organized a support group for them. Pacifist groups counseled COs, intervened with the government on their behalf, and aided noncooperators who protested prison conditions. The War Resisters League especially fought for radical pacifists when their militant actions got them into trouble with the authorities.

Some COs accepted alternative service gladly, at first. They thought the camps would operate on a high spiritual plane, guided by the sponsoring church groups. But for many it was simply making the best of a bad situation. The conscription law had grabbed them by the neck and forced them to do a job. They had no choice but the camps, the army, or prison. The element of compulsion contaminated or corrupted the whole experience. They began to feel it was a mistake to compromise this way with conscription. To go into the CPS camps meant accepting the theory that the individual is at the government's disposal. It was forced service they were doing, whatever you might call it. One CO pointed out that, while the gangster Lepke Gurrah was electrocuted by the government because he killed, COs were condemned to forced labor or prison because they *refused* to kill.

After this experience, few peace seekers said they would take the same path again. The Catholic CO Gordon Zahn, after serving four years in a camp, concluded the CPS "was punitive in practice and intent, an experiment in the democratic *suppression* of a dissident religious minority in time of war."

What helped pacifists in these years was a new focus on Gandhi's use of nonviolent resistance as a force for social change. The Indian leader advised building decentralized committees grounded in truth, justice, poverty, and mutual aid. He encouraged the use of mass civil disobedience and noncooperation when the state interfered with constructive programs. By 1940 Gandhi's ideas and experience were influencing American pacifists. They formed committees called colonies or ashrams, where they shared all possessions and a disciplined way of life anchored to Christian principles. There they discussed Gandhi's views and began to use nonviolent

Mahatma Gandhi adopted some of Thoreau's ideas on civil disobedience when he launched campaigns of nonviolent resistance
to bring about social change in South Africa and then in India.
From Gandhi's experience American pacifists learned to use
mass civil disobedience in the struggle for peace and civil rights.

tactics against racial discrimination and for improving their neighborhoods. The Newark Commune in the heart of the city's ghetto also took actions for peace during the war, protesting the deliberate saturation bombing of German and Japanese cities and the U.S. refusal to open its doors to Jewish refugees. Its ideas and actions heralded the coming civil rights movement. Such communities became centers for COs during the war.

CHAPTER FOURTEEN

Staying Number One

World War II made an enormous difference in how the United States defines and pursues its national interest. True, since its birth the United States has engaged in wars of one kind or another. But these were sporadic interventions of a scale and frequency very different from military history since 1940.

To organize for World War II, the United States underwent a bureaucratic revolution that made war the main business of government. Given a variety of incentives to produce, big business overwhelmed the enemy with its productive power. In the process, a permanent war economy developed. Business and the military knitted together a profitable network of relationships that became the channel for the substantial military production that extended into the postwar world. It was part of the deep organizational changes that secured the dominant position of the national security agencies in the federal government.

The military services and their officer corps grew astronomically. The barriers between "political" and "military" functions of government went down as the military got deeper and deeper into politics. Presidents came to rely on the military professionals to interpret for them major matters of foreign and military policy.

At the end of World War II, U.S. military forces were deployed almost everywhere, controlling over four hundred bases around the world. While some bases were given back, most were retained and still others were acquired. Their military value declined with the birth of the intercontinental nuclear missile. Still, they were kept to show the flag or to exert political influence on the home governments. America now aspired to the "responsibilities of world leadership," so federal funds continued to be poured into armaments and bases abroad even after peace returned. "We are the number one nation," President Lyndon B. Johnson would say in the 1960s, "and we are going to stay the number one nation."

The war had changed America in many other ways. Organized labor had shared in the great economic gains of the war and had become part of the establishment team. It offered no independent or critical view of foreign policy. The universities were mobilized into the wartime scientific complex, and given huge subsidies, they, too, became instruments of the state. As for the general public, almost all had enjoyed the benefits of a wartime economy. Yes, 296,000 Americans died in battle, and 680,000 suffered wounds from enemy fire. But for most of the remaining 150 million citizens, the war had meant more money in the pocket and more goods to spend it on.

The Allied crusade in what seemed the most just of wars had enabled many to ignore the evils of war itself and to whip up a war fever. "We must hate with every fiber of our being," Lieutenant General Lesley J. McNair had told the U.S. ground forces he was training. "We must lust for battle; our object in life must be to kill; we must scheme night and day to kill."

The media had joined the military in instilling hatred. Racial prejudice flared on the pages of the press. *Time* magazine called the Japanese troops "rodents" and asked for their extermination. Admiral William F. Halsey boasted in a newsreel that "we are drowning and burning the bestial apes all over the Pacific." *The New York Times* carried an ad featuring a Japanese face with the headline "Rat Poison Wanted." The process of dehumanizing the enemy so you could more easily kill him was similar to Hitler's labeling the Jews "lice" and "vermin" as he sent them to the gas chambers.

The obliteration bombing of civilian populations in German and Japanese cities had gone almost unnoticed. A combination of explosive and incendiary bombs often created raging firestorms that took huge tolls of lives in scores of cities. The American press and the church had not protested. It had been accepted as a normal way to win a war.

It was logical, then, to use America's new secret weapon, the atomic bomb, on the people of Hiroshima and Nagasaki. Evidence recently disclosed has convinced many that the atomic bomb did shorten the war. But "the larger question of mass destruction of civilians by bombings, whether conventional or nuclear, remains unanswered," writes the Christian historian Ronald A. Wells. "In a 'just' war should such a draconian policy ever have been implemented in the first place? A Christian would be hard pressed to answer this affirmatively."

One myth replaced another in the course of that war. People had believed that peace, not war, was the normal state of human affairs. Now they were told the world was fated to be always at war. To a Sunday-school class of eight-year-olds, General George S. Patton said, "You are the soldiers and nurses of the next war. There will be another war. There always has been."

Was General Patton right? The socio-military analyst Richard J. Barnet writes:

Staying number one is a struggle for permanent victory. . . . In the pursuit of permanent victory the United States has engaged in a form of permanent war. Since 1940 this country has mobilized and maintained the most powerful military force in the world. In this period American forces have waged a global war and two large land wars (Korea and Vietnam). Since 1945 the US has also conducted a major military campaign or a paramilitary CIA operation in a former colonial or dependent country on an average of once every 18 months—Greece (1948), Korea (1951–1953), Iran (1953), Guatemala (1954), Indonesia (1958), Lebanon (1958), Laos (1960), Cuba (1961), Congo (1964), British Guiana (1964), Dominican Republic (1965), and of course Vietnam (1950–1972).

An American flotilla dominates the Mediterranean and the Far Pacific. American bombers loaded with hydrogen bombs and missiles concealed in concrete are poised to annihilate within minutes any society in the world. The American nuclear arsenal holds the equivalent of ten thousand tons of TNT for every man, woman, and child on earth. To pay for this the American economy has been on a war footing since 1940. Each year between fifty and seventy cents of every tax dollar goes to support this military establishment.

Pacifists from their special perspective came to the same conclusion. Said the Quaker Clarence Pickett: "We have emerged from World War II more fearful, more anxious, more committed to the use of physical violence for protection, than we have ever been before." In the eerie glow of Hiroshima, however, some saw the end of the military road. Unless we are insane, humankind must draw back from the rim of the abyss. Nuclear weapons swung many back to pacifism. Humane scientists did their best to prevent a nuclear arms race. Einstein said that "non-cooperation in military matters should be an essential moral principle for all true scientists."

The peaceful uses of atomic energy were stressed by defenders of nuclear power, in the hope of defusing the antinuclear movement. Not until decades later, however, did the public begin to lose faith in atomic energy when disasters at nuclear plants and the intractable problem of disposing of nuclear wastes choked off its growth.

But nuclear arms continued to proliferate. Soon several nations besides the United States and the Soviet Union found the way to make or buy them. This frightened people into realizing that they must work to create a world society—not fifty or five hundred years hence, but *now*. At first the United Nations created at war's end held out hope of peaceful solutions to conflict. But it soon became clear the U.N. was only an alliance of powers who refused to give up any sovereignty. One group competed against another with few or no restraints. The atomic threat made nationalism and sovereignty seem foolish, yet dozens of new nations came into being, each prizing its sovereignty.

A young generation of pacifists took hold of nonviolent resistance as the best means to halt war and fight injustice. They saw the method as both a political and moral instrument. Would it have worked against Hitler? Perhaps if enough Germans, early on, had adopted and used it. But they did not. They showed a frightful capacity to justify the inhumanity of Auschwitz, as Americans did to justify Hiroshima. Was acceptance of the wholesale destruction of human life evidence of a general corruption of the spirit?

The fascist enemy of World War II became the rationale for rejecting pacifism. To many, Hitler signified a worse horror than the huge losses of combat. The evil of totalitarianism was soon transferred to its communist form. Many Americans became converted to the belief that their security against the threat of communism rested on superior military power. Politics was oversimplified into the struggle between Good and Evil, between the Free World and Communism. Americans felt morally superior to the enemy, quick to tell others what to do about the threat and to intervene wherever America wished. Pacifism was, and often still is, seen as standing in the way of the United States' preparing for the coming war. Pacifists were accused of "seeking peace at any price."

Concern for national security became paramount in politics. Fear of hostile powers, of revolutionary ferment, of internal subversion, drove political leaders to seek safety in military preparedness. That the nations suffered 80 million casualties in World War II did not turn them from this path. For the sake of security through violence, the United States developed with incredible speed the nuclear means to exterminate its enemies. War for the first time became a threat to the literal survival of the species. Peace became defined as armed deterrence.

An expanding national security state was a huge obstacle for peace activists to overcome. What made it worse was the rising cold war between the United States and the Soviet Union. Wartime cooperation gave way to confrontation between the two superpowers. International tensions sharpened security fears and spurred the expansion of the military. In 1947 President Truman declared he would defend Greece and Turkey as well as all "free peoples" anywhere resisting communist subversion within or attack from without. The new "Truman Doctrine" meant, he said, that American foreign policy had "now declared that wherever aggression, direct or indirect, threatened the peace, the security of the United States was involved."

The Soviet Union on its side tightened its control over Eastern Europe, and in 1948 it engineered a communist coup in Czechoslovakia and blockaded Berlin. The next year Mao Zedong's Red Army seized power in China. World politics was frozen into two blocs of contending powers—communist and anticommunist—with each seeking to extend its influence into every corner of the globe.

The peace movement was discouraged. It was labeled red inspired here at home. And what chance did pacifists have to exert influence in the increasing number of totalitarian countries? Then in 1950 Wisconsin Senator Joseph R. McCarthy launched his anticommunist crusade. It strangled free thought for years to come and drove the fearful out of any organization or action that might be labeled liberal or radical. "Politics in Cold War America," wrote one historian, "veered into a fogbank of rightist repression. After the early 1950s only the lonely professed to doubt the need for a vigilant security state and the danger of subversives within and enemies without."

The draft law adopted in 1940 expired in 1947, and plans for a new version were announced. Pacifists saw the news as a sinister step "making security impossible and war inevitable." The National Council Against Conscription was formed, but the law was adopted in 1948.

A new generation of radical pacifists had been shaped by their wartime experience in resisting racial segregation and government authority in the camps and prisons. The old orthodox, passive pacifists gave way to them. They created such groups as Peacemakers and the Committee for Nonviolent Action, both in the pattern of Gandhi's Indian ashrams. They believed individual resistance was the best hope, the only hope, in the face of the huge institutional forces pushing the world to oblivion. Their goal was to unite the noncommunist left for nonviolent action for peace and economic and racial justice. It was the only way to strive for human dignity and survival in a country gearing for war. They failed to get very far, but they would not give up the attempt to overcome injustice and prevent another world war.

Both as individuals and in groups they took a variety of peace actions. They refused to pay federal income taxes and after 1948 resisted the draft. By early 1949, eighty-seven men had been arrested for not registering and forty-two were sent to prison for sixty days to four years. Larry Gara, a history professor, was jailed for having "counseled, aided, and abetted" a student in refusing to register. The judge's decision made it illegal to use free speech to advocate draft resistance. (Gara had already served two separate sentences as a CO in World War II.)

Do what they could, pacifist leaders rapidly lost their influence with the traditional sources of their strength. Most anticommunist liberals backed Truman's cold war policies and bigger military budgets. The socialists were few and feeble. Students ignored social issues to train for careers. The church seemed asleep. The unions were politically split and on the defensive against management. Middle-class women lost their jobs to returning veterans and withdrew into domestic concerns. The peace seekers were left without any visible means of support.

So when the next war came, in Korea, only weak voices were raised against it. The Korean War had its roots in the long Japanese occupation of the peninsula. When the Japanese surrendered in 1945, American and Soviet troops occupied Korea and divided the country at the thirty-eighth parallel. The cold war froze the temporary boundary, and two competing regions developed. The Soviets equipped the North Korean army, and in 1950 its troops crossed the thirty-eighth parallel to "liberate" the south. The U.N. branded the action as aggression and asked its members to help repel the attack. Fifteen nations sent troops, but most of the forces were American and South Korean. Truman sent in troops without asking Congress to declare war, setting an ominous precedent for the "presidential wars" to come. Truman's aim was a "limited" war, only to defend South Korea, not to unite all Korea (which might have started a third world war).

A treaty ended the war in July 1953. U.S. casualties were about 34,000 killed in battle, 20,000 dead of other causes, and 100,000 wounded.

During the war, the national security state flourished. Military budgets quadrupled, and the size of the armed forces tripled. Draft policies protected the educated class. Student deferments were much easier to get than in World War II. (Korea, too, proved a poor man's war.) Men of higher social class who did serve usually got assignments in safe places.

There was a record rate of men classified as COs. They came from the peace churches and beyond, and in greater numbers. In World War II COs numbered four per ten thousand; in the Korean War it reached thirteen per ten thousand. Although the war did not have the popular support of World War II, desertion rates were lower. As losses mounted toward the end of the war, about half the American people decided we should have stayed out.

CHAPTER FIFTEEN

Disaster in Vietnam

Relieved to see the Korean War over at last, Americans turned again to their private affairs. The peace movement—small and isolated—was barely able to stay alive. Pacifism was marking time, its leaders wondering whether a world without war was really possible.

The silence about the dangers of the cold war was broken in 1955 when Einstein and the British philosopher Bertrand Russell issued an appeal to the world signed by many of the world's great scientists. They addressed themselves to

all the powerful governments of the world in the earnest hope that they may agree to allow their citizens to survive. We are speaking not as members of this or that nation, continent or creed, but as human beings, members of the species man, whose continued existence is in doubt. . . . Shall we choose death, because we cannot forget our quarrels? We appeal, as human beings, to human beings: Remember your humanity and forget the rest.

A week later, a conference of fifty-two Nobel laureates issued its own statement. It called on all nations to "renounce force as a final resort of policy," warning that "if they are not prepared to do this, they will cease to exist."

That year the Quakers published an influential study, *Speak Truth to Power*. It was not content simply to indict reliance on military power. Rather, it pointed out what "considerable agreement" there was on the "positive requirements" for peace—a basic attack upon world poverty, an end to colonialism, the development of world organization, and disarmament. But why don't we *act* on these policies? the Quakers asked. Instead, the arms race goes on, the U.N. weakens, economic aid declines, and the United States supports undemocratic governments determined to keep things as they are.

The answer, said the Quakers, lies "in the nature and meaning of Twentieth Century commitment to organized mass violence . . . in the poisonous doctrine that *our* ends justify any means." These are "not evils of which the Communists alone are guilty—they are a part of the main drift of our time."

If the United States fails to act constructively, the Quakers went on, then the individual has to look to himself.

Each man is the source of freedom within himself. He can say "No" whenever he sees himself compromised. Speak Truth to Power *says this "No" to the war machine and to the immoral claims of power wherever they exist as the essential moral and political act of our time. It calls on all men to say "Yes" to courageous non-violence, which alone can overcome injustice, persecution, and tyranny.*

Almost at that moment a dynamic social movement flared up in Montgomery, Alabama, around a pacifist ideal advocated by the young black minister Dr. Martin Luther King, Jr. The city's blacks carried out a successful bus boycott that ended segregated seating. Against the brutal aggression of the racists, massive nonviolent resistance to injustice emerged as the means of advancing the nationwide struggle for civil rights. The path marked out long before by Thoreau and more recently by Gandhi—justice without violence—was rediscovered by Dr.

In college, Martin Luther King, Jr., was "fascinated by Thoreau's idea of refusing to cooperate with an evil system." He adopted the nonviolent idea to launch a civil rights crusade. King's strategy of direct action was taken up by the peace movement as the way to oppose nuclear armaments and war.

King as the course that could lead to change. (Dr. King in 1964 was awarded the Nobel Prize for peace in recognition of his championship of nonviolence.)

The civil rights crusade and the danger of radioactive nuclear fallout gave the peace movement fresh stimulus. Dr. King's strategy of direct action was taken up by aroused citizens as a peaceable way to attack both racism and armaments. Pacifists in 1957 formed the National Committee for a Sane Nuclear Policy (usually known as Sane). It tried to bring pressure for suspending atomic testing at once, and for gradual general disarmament and international control of atomic development. The Committee for Non-Violent Action (CNVA) adopted civil disobedience methods to invade U.S. missile installations and risk death by walking into restricted nuclear test sites while bombs were being exploded. The radical pacifists hoped such militant actions would jolt the American people into facing up to the twin threats of militarism and war. CNVA organized a San Francisco-to-Moscow Walk for Peace in the early 1960s, and at New London, Connecticut, members leaped aboard nuclear submarines and urged shipyard workers to refuse to build submarines carrying nuclear missiles. Their efforts brought publicity but little more. It was hard to persuade workers to give up their jobs for an ideal.

During the October 1962 crisis over the installation of Soviet missiles on Cuban soil, Americans and Russians looked World War III in the face. The pacifists were appalled by the popular conclusions drawn from the ending of the crisis: that if the United States had gone to the brink and not fallen over, then why couldn't it do this again and again and again?

By now fresh recruits to the peace movement were coming in from the universities—both students and faculty—and from women off the campus. The Student Peace Union (SPU) appeared on campuses after a decade of student inaction. Local women's peace action groups organized into the national Women Strike for Peace (WSP) to mobilize women—young mothers especially—to protest the nuclear arms race. Activists refused to take shelter during civil defense drills because the drills offered no safety against nuclear attack and only made people believe that war was inevitable and nuclear attack survivable. Such civil disobedience rose to new levels across the country. In 1962 the WSP could rally fifty thousand women in sixty cities against the nuclear arms race and in favor of mutual disarmament, while the SPU could bring seven thousand students to Washington to demonstrate against atmospheric testing and civil defense programs.

Ten years had passed since the Korean War, and again the United States was becoming deeply involved in the affairs of a country remote from its own borders—Vietnam. Peace leaders feared that entanglement would produce another Korean War or even worse. Under President John F. Kennedy, they saw the Pentagon budget rise to $50 billion, the armed forces to 3 million men, through the draft and volunteers, and the nuclear arsenal to an explosive power 1.5 million times greater than that of the bomb that destroyed Hiroshima.

On the other hand, Kennedy's administration established an Arms Control and Disarmament Agency and in 1963 reached agreement with the Russians on a nuclear test ban treaty. Reassured by these steps, the peace movement slowed down, turning its energies into the heated civil rights struggle.

What the movement missed was the change in military strategy taking place in the sixties. While Kennedy tried to lessen the chance of a nuclear holocaust after the Cuban missile crisis, he at the same time built up the military's capacity to wage "conventional" wars. Small counterinsurgency forces would be relied on "to put out fires" abroad. At this time, also, America took it as its mission to crush social revolution in the "underdeveloped world." No matter how corrupt, repressive, and hated a "friendly" regime actually was, it was our obligation (following the Truman Doctrine) to keep a so-called "free" regime in power.

This notion would become known as the "falling row of dominoes" theory. One "free world" nation falling would lead to the fall of another next to it, and then another and another and another, until the world would be taken over by the communists or destroyed in a nuclear holocaust. Each domino in danger was viewed as merely a pawn in a larger communist game played by either the Soviet Union or China.

In the case of Vietnam, the domino experts like Richard Nixon warned that the fate of Vietnam would be the fate of all Southeast Asia. Let Vietnam fall, and Laos, Cambodia, Thailand, Burma, and Indonesia would topple after it. Then we'd have to fight a big war to save the Philippines, and Japan would be pulled toward neutralism or even into the communist orbit. The Pacific would become a "Red sea," and soon afterward Australia would fall to China's aggression. (As we'll see, the Reagan Administration would apply this domino theory to Central America.)

It would take more pages than there is room in this book to explore in detail the complex history of the Vietnam War. It was the century's longest and most controversial war. It lasted from 1945 to 1975—thirty years! In that time, 2.8 million U.S. troops went to Vietnam, and 58,000 Americans and at least 2 million Vietnamese died. It proved to be America's most disastrous military adventure.

Vietnam is an ancient country with a recorded history of more than two thousand years. Much of it is the story of resistance to the neighboring Chinese. The endless struggle for independence shaped Vietnam's culture. It made the people tough and durable, imbued with a fierce nationalist spirit.

From the nineteenth century, Vietnam had been a colony of France. When the Japanese began World War II, they overran Indochina and took control of Vietnam, ruling it through the French, however. As the Japanese neared defeat in 1945, an independent Vietnamese republic, with its capital in Hanoi in the north, was proclaimed by Ho Chi Minh, the Communist leader; he had directed guerrilla activity during the war.

The French, who returned to Indochina late in 1945, gained control of the southern part of Vietnam. Fighting broke out in northern Vietnam, too, and Ho went underground to lead a guerrilla war against the new colonialism. In response to a French request, the United States in 1950 began providing economic and military aid to them in Indochina. It jumped to $500 million in 1951 and leaped higher annually from then on.

The Vietnamese won a decisive military victory

over the French in 1954, and talk of a negotiated settlement began. But the United States opposed it. President Eisenhower feared it would hand over not only Vietnam but the whole of Southeast Asia to communism. The "falling row of dominoes" theory again. Finally, the two Vietnam regimes agreed to peace talks at Geneva in which the United States, France, Britain, the USSR, China, Cambodia, and Laos also took part. The Geneva Agreements of July 1954 ended France's sixty-year domination over Indochina. The decisions at the conference included dividing Vietnam temporarily along the seventeenth parallel until general elections to be held in 1956 could reunify the country, and establishing Laos and Cambodia as independent nations. The United States refused to sign the agreements but promised to refrain from using force to disturb the settlement.

America took over France's role, and gave large amounts of aid to the newly created South Vietnam regime. When that government refused to allow the promised elections in 1956, guerrilla warfare broke out. The resistance came not primarily from communists but from members of religious sects, the Buddhists, and all other critics of the repressive government.

While civil war racked the south, the north's economy was being rebuilt with Soviet and Chinese aid, and Ho began to help the guerrillas (the Vietcong) in the south.

Although South Vietnam's government was never popular among its own people, it was praised to the skies in the United States. Senator John F. Kennedy called it "the cornerstone of the Free World in Southeast Asia, the keystone in the arch, the finger in the dike." He warned that if the "red tide of Communism" should pour into it, the rest of Asia would be threatened.

In August 1954 Washington assumed the burden of defending South Vietnam and sent in a CIA team to begin covert operations against the guerrilla forces. Military advisers arrived to train the South Vietnamese army. But no matter how much help the government got (most of it disappearing into a swamp of corruption), things got worse and worse.

When Kennedy became President in 1961, he resolved to meet what he saw as the threat of communist subversion of the underdeveloped nations. He raised America's commitment of troops to fifteen thousand men by 1963. Much of this was done secretly, because it violated the Geneva agreements. The aid program tried to build a strong army in the South so it could overcome the guerrillas and resist a possible invasion from the north.

The United States focused narrowly on military

matters; it missed the crucial importance of political affairs in trying to build a strong nation. South Vietnam had a constitution that provided for a president and a legislature elected by popular vote. But President Ngo Dinh Diem of South Vietnam believed he knew what was best for the people and ruled them like a dictator.

With the help of American men and weapons, the government forces waged war against the Vietcong. But by 1963 they were losing badly. And many Americans began to feel disturbed at the methods of warfare. It was hard to tell the difference between civilians and the guerrillas fighting in the jungle, and the South Vietnamese government forces did not try very hard to make distinctions. They killed civilians—men, women, and children—using the most brutal of modern weapons. They bombed and strafed villages, they burned people with napalm and defoliated forests with chemicals. Later, as the Americans took over much of the fighting, they used the same methods.

Finally the United States deserted Diem, and in November 1963 he and members of his family were killed in a coup led by his own generals and encouraged by the United States. (Three weeks later President Kennedy was assassinated, too.)

American pacifists had all along criticized the priority successive Presidents gave to defeating communism. Washington refused to face the realities. In 1964 the War Resisters League pointed out that it was useless to try to shore up a corrupt and artificially created regime. It warned that air power would destroy civilians, too, because the Vietcong could not be spotted. Extending the war to cut off supply lines from North Vietnam or China would be futile, since the Vietcong could keep going with arms and supplies captured from South Vietnamese troops. "We are trapped," the WRL concluded, "in a situation where no traditional victory can be won in South Vietnam regardless of how many more troops and how much more equipment are poured in."

It would take another ten years for the United States to admit the truth of this warning.

President Lyndon B. Johnson came to office inheriting an even worse situation than Kennedy had acquired from Eisenhower. Johnson ran as a "peace" candidate against Barry Goldwater in 1964, painting his Republican opponent almost as a mad dog panting for war, while at the same time the President was secretly approving covert operations in Vietnam that would include air and sea action. In August, during the campaign, an alleged attack by the enemy against U.S. naval units operating in North Vietnamese waters gave Johnson the excuse for the first U.S.

bombing of North Vietnam. Thus, on August 5, 1964, the United States directly entered the Vietnam War, without declaration. From Congress Johnson got his Tonkin Gulf resolution approving his action—and further actions. It gave the President what amounted to a blank check—the power "to take all necessary measures to repel any armed attack against the forces of the United States and to prevent further aggression."

Johnson used this resolution to justify a major buildup of American forces in Southeast Asia. He was going to face this little country of 17 million people with the huge power of America. They would be too scared to fight on, and would be ready to compromise. Showing our strength would thus *prevent* war. Instead, the United States was plunged into an almost endless war of enormous proportions.

Johnson took the Tonkin Gulf resolution to guarantee public support for virtually any military action. An opinion poll showed Johnson's personal popularity soaring from 42 to 72 percent overnight. And in November, Johnson, as the "moderate" candidate, won a landslide victory over the "bloodthirsty" Goldwater.

The President mistook the signs. Even before his election the first notable protest against the war occurred, at the University of California at Berkeley.

And three prominent political figures who had supported U.S. policy in Vietnam—John Kenneth Galbraith and Senators William J. Fulbright and Robert F. Kennedy—now turned against it. These were the first hints of dissent that would mount higher and higher.

Johnson rapidly increased troop strength and launched a campaign of heavy bombing over North Vietnam. Instead of giving up in defeat, however, Ho sent more men south. American generals argued for more men and planes to enable them to win the war. Johnson usually gave them what they asked for, and by 1966 half a million troops were in Vietnam.

The result? The foundations of South Vietnam's society were largely destroyed. Villages, food production, family life were wiped out. Much of the population had fled the countryside to live in slums near army bases or near cities like Saigon. It was colonialism new-style, this time American. The high-sounding moral claims of the United States for entering the war were wrecked by the unlimited aerial warfare that destroyed the small country. This was no just war by any standard.

CHAPTER SIXTEEN

The Resistance

The massive bombing assaults on Vietnam began to galvanize Americans into opposition to the war. The first major demonstration against it took place in New York and a dozen other cities late in 1964. The protesters issued "an appeal to the American conscience" that urged an immediate cease-fire and the earliest possible withdrawal of U.S. troops. In 1965 three people—Alice Herz, a survivor of Nazi terror; Quaker Norman Morrison; and Catholic Worker volunteer Roger LaPorte—burned themselves to death in protest against the war. That spring Students for a Democratic Society (SDS) led a March on Washington to end the war. In June pacifists conducted a "speak-out" against the war on the steps of the Pentagon, and "teach-ins"—round-the-clock meetings on Vietnam—swept the college campuses and woke students to the truth about Vietnam.

There were dozens of ways people chose to oppose the war. They picketed and marched; they wore buttons and carried slogans; they wrote books, articles, plays, and poems; they attended teach-ins and poetry read-ins; they signed ads and wrote letters to the editor. And they took to more dramatic methods of nonviolent resistance. They staged a sitdown in Washington in which hundreds of people were arrested. On the West Coast they tried to stop trains arriving at Oakland with soldiers assigned to Vietnam.

Soon the movement was gathering together people of many differing political views who agreed only on the need to get America out of Vietnam. There were the traditional pacifists, the peace church members, the respectable liberals, the socialists, the communists, and their more extreme radical splinters. Few had ever agreed with, or worked together with, one another before, but now they stressed unity of action against the war.

Draft card burnings began in the fall of 1965. A young Catholic Worker, David Miller, was the first to burn his draft card in a demonstration at the Induction Center in New York. His act of defiance

A student in Chicago burns his draft card in front of an induction center to protest against the war in Vietnam. Such public acts of defiance brought jail sentences, but the antiwar movement continued to grow.

got enormous publicity, and Congress passed a law making it a felony, equal to draft refusal, to destroy a draft card. Miller was sentenced to two and a half years in prison. There were more such burnings. At one ceremony, A. J. Muste told the crowd,

Some young men here are about to burn their draft cards in public. I am aware that if any considerable number of young men and other citizens were to take this stand, the U.S. could not wage war. I think that would be a glorious day in the life of this nation and in the history of mankind.

Accused by the government of lawless behavior, the pacifists replied, "The real lawlessness at loose in the world today is that of the President and his advisors who violate international law and outrage the moral values of all mankind by their actions in Vietnam." The government prosecuted fewer than fifty draft-card burners; about forty of them were convicted.

Not content with the negative aspects of the anti-war movement, some young people in the sixties tried to bring a positive joy to peace demonstrations. They wanted not just to oppose war but to celebrate a new and different kind of life. Many chose to drop out of a society they felt gave all its energy to war and production for war. The most influential voice they listened to was Paul Goodman's. In his books and campus lectures, he promised life and love and rejected military violence, sexual conformity, and racial hatred. "In a society that is cluttered, overcentralized and overadministered," he wrote, "we should aim at simplification, decentralization, and decontrol."

Once, in 1967, Goodman was asked to speak at the State Department to a National Security Industrial Association conference. He said exactly what he thought:

Our abundant society is at present simply deficient in many of the most elementary objective opportunities and worthwhile goals that could make growing up possible. It is lacking . . . in honest public speech . . . in the opportunity to be useful. It thwarts aptitude and creates stupidity. It corrupts ingenuous patriotism. It corrupts the fine arts. It shackles science. It dampens animal ardor. It discourages the religious convictions of Justification and Vocation. It has no Honor. It has no Community.

Uneasy as the war had made a great many Americans, most still saw Vietnam as an unhappy mistake, a departure from American tradition. They gave the United States and the Administration the benefit of the doubt. The more radical pacifists, such as A. J. Muste, viewed Vietnam as a logical outgrowth of America's addiction to violence and the belief that

America was the greatest and the best nation on earth. Muste tried to get Americans to see themselves as people abroad saw their country—an aggressive power determined to dictate to the rest of the world how they should live. Instead of facing up to this, he said, U.S. leaders carried out foreign policy in a spirit of constant self-justification and self-praise.

The public outcry for a change in policy was joined by eminent scholars who published an open letter in *The New York Times* expressing strong dissent from the war. Opposition began to rise within the Congress and among other federal figures. Johnson felt the mounting pressure. As one observer wrote:

Street demonstrations were frequent during 1966. The slightest provocation was enough to bring people into the streets to picket a dinner addressed by Secretary of State Rusk, to block traffic in protest of renewed bombing of North Vietnam, to block military recruiters on campus, to sit-in at the Dow Chemical offices protesting its manufacture of napalm, to distribute anti-draft leaflets in the early morning hours at induction centers urging young men to refuse to be drafted and offering advice on how to stay out—there was a demonstration for every occasion. The main purpose . . . was to make the anti-war movement visible to the American public and to make the media, which was overwhelmingly in support of the war and opposed to criticism of government policy, acknowledge that an opposition

241

did exist, that it was vocal and could disrupt the status quo if provoked far enough.

Draft-age students were coming in ever greater numbers to the pacifist groups to seek advice on what to do. Cases of defection from the military because of revulsion against the carnage in Vietnam now came to light. Men who had entered service changed their minds during training or later and refused to continue serving. The most famous such case was that of the Fort Hood Three—three soldiers who refused to serve in Vietnam. It went to court-martial in a test of whether the government could constitutionally compel GIs who were not pacifists but refused to fight in Vietnam to do so. The defense believed it involved the right of men in service to think for themselves, to discuss the issues of the war, and to refuse to obey orders to commit what they felt to be war crimes.

But during trial the defense lawyers were denied the right to argue that the Vietnam War was illegal. The outcome was inevitable. The three soldiers were sentenced to prison and given dishonorable discharges.

The issue of conscientious objection went to the courts again in the sixties. Two questions were raised—about the nonreligious, or secular, objector and about the political, selective objector. The first argued that his opposition to war was just as solid for being based on ethical rather than religious grounds. The second argued that his protest was valid, although it was not against all wars but one particular war. The courts gave varying decisions on these issues. But in 1970 (*Welsh v. United States*) the Supreme Court held that the CO provision in the law "exempts from military service all those whose conscience spurred by deeply held moral, ethical, or religious beliefs, would give them no rest or peace if they allowed themselves to become a part of the instrument of war." It ruled out COs "whose beliefs are not deeply held and those whose objection to war does not rest at all upon moral, ethical, or religious principle but instead rests solely upon considerations of polity, pragmatism, or expediency." This last sentence meant that objection to one war in particular—selective objection—was not allowed. Such a principle would run against the need of the country to defend itself.

Some jurists did not agree. They believed that denial of exemption from military service for selective objectors is unconstitutional. Massachusetts Judge Charles Wyzanski wrote that a selective CO's claim

is not appreciably lessened if his belief relates not to war in general, but to a particular type of war. Indeed, a selective conscientious objector might reflect a more discriminating study of the problem, a more sensitive conscience, and a deeply spiritual understanding.

A black CO, interviewed in prison, explains why he refused to serve:

I believe in brotherhood and loving people. I suppose that on an individual basis it's a natural thing for a man to protect himself as a matter of self-defense, but it becomes a different thing, even for self-defense, when it's institutionalized. I think that military institutions have disunited and separated men, and that is contrary to a basic belief of mine. I couldn't take a life just for that. That other man might be my brother. I don't think any war is ever justified. While I do believe that I'm against war in general, this one, particularly, just doesn't have anything to do with anything I believe in.

Throughout the Vietnam War there were many men who refused to register for the draft or to be inducted. The list of such men grew larger and larger as the war went on, from some eighteen thousand in 1964 to forty thousand in 1970 and sixty thousand in 1971. The first mass refusal of the draft occurred in the spring of 1967 in New York's Central Park. During an antiwar rally of hundreds of thousands, 175 men burned their draft cards in a collec-

244

tive refusal to serve. After that, thousands of others took part around the country in draft-card burnings or in draft-card turn-ins. It was plain that going to jail rather than fighting was no longer thought to be cowardly. Maybe the "soft" pacifists were more honest and realistic than the "tough" generals?

The implied threat of the resistance was that if Washington escalated the war and called for more men, thousands would not serve. During the Vietnam era there were 172,000 COs. Made to do alternative service, they worked for two years at low-paid jobs beyond easy distance from home. Their service was often so casually checked that about 50,000 COs dropped out before completing their duty. Only a thousand were convicted of that offense.

To support noncooperation with the draft, the movement set up GI coffeehouses near military bases. It sneaked antiwar leaflets into the training camps and gave deserters refuge while organizing legal aid or helping them flee to another country. People sheltered GI resisters much as abolitionists had organized the Underground Railroad for runaway slaves. By war's end there were nearly a hundred thousand military deserters or draft evaders. Most were in Canada, with some in Sweden, France, and other Western European countries, many of which granted legal asylum.

It began with individual dissent in the early years, 1965–67. The Fort Hood Three were but one example of that first phase. Dr. Howard Levy, who refused to train Green Beret medics, was an even more famous case. He was sentenced to three years at hard labor plus a dishonorable discharge as the army tried to discourage others from following his example.

In 1968 an underground press edited by GIs began to grow. Scores of such papers appeared in the United States, in Germany, and at bases throughout the world, including Vietnam. They provided a forum for dissenters and for grievances against the way the military treated the GIs. Men like Captain Levy and the Fort Hood Three were no longer standing alone. Such actions as theirs won increasing support in the ranks.

Soon there were mutinies—over ten major ones in the field during the war. And AWOLs, deserters, disobeying of orders. The military brass struck hard at the protest. Going beyond the usual punishments of KP and extra sentry duty, they gave men transfers, courts-martial, and prison sentences. Military intelligence agents infested the camps to spy on suspected dissenters.

But the dissent went on, and spread. Appalling signs of disintegrating morale could be seen in the high figures of desertion rates, drug addiction, and the "fragging" or assassination of officers. These symptoms were true for the entire military, both inside and outside of Vietnam.

Another form of dissent by servicemen was the seeking of CO status. This meant making a moral stand against the war; it was vastly harder to make your case within the military. Yet in 1971 alone four thousand men took this course. Over 75 percent of the servicemen who asked CO status in 1972 were granted it.

Talking to those who condemned dissenters, whether in or out of uniform, Senator Mark Hatfield, an evangelical spokesman, explained what dissent stood for:

Those who question the loyalty of the dissenters often subscribe to a perverted patriotism, a patriotism based on flag-waving, heart-pounding commitment to "my country right or wrong." I would counsel these people not to confuse patriotism with blind endorsement of bad policy. Responsible dissenters are sincerely convinced that our policies in Vietnam are wrong and that they must be corrected if the best interests of the United States are to be served. Just like the super-patriots, we want what is best for our country and the world, but we don't think that our present policies, or a red-white-and-blue obeisance to these policies for the sake of "national unity," serves the long-term interests of the United States. Believing this, we have a duty *to speak out, to try and change bad policy.*

Hatfield went on to call the domino theory false. This was no war instigated by an outside power— China or Russia. From the start it had been a civil war among the Vietnamese. The claim that the United States was defending the freedom of Southeast Asia was false, too, he said. He showed that the South Vietnamese were denied freedom of the press, of speech, of assembly, of petition. The Saigon government used Gestapo methods against its own people and conducted dishonest elections.

All through the war, the U.S. government worked hard to crush dissent. Draft cases were given top priority in federal court, and resistance figures such as Dr. Benjamin Spock, the Rev. William Sloane Coffin, and Fathers Philip and Daniel Berrigan were prosecuted and some of them jailed. Sentences for draft evasion lengthened during the peak war years. The average prison term for a convicted evader was twenty-one months at first; it rose to over thirty-seven months in 1968, and near the end, in 1973, it dropped to about eighteen months. The decline came as the government observed a majority of the public turning against the war.

Although over 200,000 men were accused draft

offenders, only 25,000 were indicted. And of these, only 8,750 were convicted. Fewer than 4,000 of them spent time in prison. The turn in the public tide of opinion made prosecutors reluctant to press cases, juries reluctant to convict, and judges reluctant to impose stiff sentences.

The antidraft activists were as usual from the privileged classes—the well-to-do and the educated. Members of the big middle class didn't have to serve: By becoming perpetual college students, they could avoid the draft. Any college men who did end up in jail or in the armed forces were there by choice. There were many who felt it unfair to hide behind a student deferment. They either signed up to fight or they risked jail by opposing the draft and the war.

The poor chose not to register as their way of staying out of war. Estimates on how many did this ranged up to 2 million. About half were black. Another form of draft resistance was to refuse induction. By 1970 one half the men slated for induction did not show up. And another 11 percent, once there, refused induction. Resistance to the draft was so strong, the government could neither prosecute nor convict the overwhelming majority of cases. The United States was no longer able to place a large land force in Vietnam to carry on the war.

What went on within the armed forces was perhaps worse, from the government's point of view. Colonel Robert Heinl wrote in the *Armed Forces Journal* in June 1971: "The morale, discipline and battle-worthiness of the US Armed Forces are, with a few salient exceptions, lower and worse than at any time in this century and possibly in the history of the United States."

By 1971, a study showed, if you examined a random group of a hundred army soldiers, you'd find seven desertions, seventeen AWOLs, twenty frequent marijuana users, ten using narcotics regularly, two disciplinary discharges, eighteen lighter punishments, and twelve complaints to Congress.

In his analysis of the Vietnam era, David S. Surrey wrote:

Avoidance and resistance often carried a heavy price. We must not lose sight of the men who were channeled through deferments into professions they might not have preferred; the men who dodged Vietnam by enlisting in certain programs and who wound up serving another year as a result; the men who married or had children in order to escape the draft; the men who never registered for the draft, or did not show up for induction and spent years living in fear of knocks at the door; the deserters who stayed underground in this country; and the men who served in prisons or stockades as a result of evasion, desertion or dissent. There are also the bad paper veter-

ans who are still being denied their rights, often for beliefs no different from those of the men who escaped the draft by the class-centered deferment system.

To fight for peace and their rights, American soldiers who returned from the war organized Vietnam Veterans Against the War. It was the first time U.S. veterans had come out of battle to work against a war. This time, however, they had lost all confidence in their superiors and were convinced of the emptiness of their sacrifice. Their many demonstrations helped the antiwar movement immensely. It forced the country to face the disastrous loss of morale and effectiveness within the armed forces. Several other such groups of veterans formed, including officers, to work for peace within the military of a nation at war.

Antiwar action in the streets continued to bring pressure on Washington. The most notable example was the siege of the Pentagon in October 1967. Thousands of demonstrators marched on the building. When soldiers barred the entrance, the demonstrators sat down at the troops' feet and offered a teach-in that lasted over twenty-four hours. Hundreds were arrested and many beaten by U.S. marshals who tried to break their spirits.

At the same time, ten thousand people took part

in a Stop-the-War Week planned to shut down the Oakland Induction Center. The center was forced to close for three hours, and street traffic and normal business were disrupted for days.

Pacifists made small nonviolent raids on Selective Service offices, where they burned draft files. Although many were jailed for it, about a million files were destroyed in such widespread actions.

In the seventies, resistance by refusal to pay war taxes won more supporters. A War Tax Resistance organization was formed to study all aspects of conscientious tax refusal. It fed information and advice to over two hundred local war tax resistance centers. The movement persisted after the war, with pacifists and nonpacifists resolved not to support the huge and growing military budgets of their government.

Toward the end of the 1960s, the antiwar movement began to split into violent and nonviolent factions, pulled by the politics of various leftist groups. As some watched the United States use its military power to crush social revolution in other "underdeveloped" countries besides Vietnam, they interpreted it as aggression on behalf of powerful economic interests. At home they saw Johnson's Great Society program scuttled as all the funds were poured into Vietnam. Looking at the world through the eyes of the poor and oppressed, they believed

Religious leaders stand in silent prayer in Arlington National Cemetery on February 6, 1968, to protest the Vietnam War. (Dr. Martin Luther King, Jr., stands in the center with arms folded.)

the enemy was right here at home, not ninety or nine thousand miles away. Some activists for peace wondered, Did the world need peace? Or did it need revolution?

The once-pacifist Student Non-Violent Coordinating Committee (SNCC) rejected nonviolence and began to talk of "guerrilla war" and "liberation struggles." And SDS made a saint of Che Guevara, the revolutionary leader in Latin America. The murders of the Kennedy brothers and Martin Luther King, Jr., swept still others away from the path of nonviolent resistance.

The groups abandoning pacifism lost influence and membership. But the antiwar movement was still able to mobilize many thousands for peaceful rallies and marches. With President Richard Nixon's help. On April 20, 1970, the President abruptly ordered the invasion of Cambodia and the renewed bombing of North Vietnam. His actions unloosed a flood of antiwar demonstrations on campuses across the country. At Kent State University, on May 4, Ohio National Guardsmen shot down thirteen students, killing four, and the next day Mississippi police killed two more students at Jackson State College. Enraged by the brutal show of state power, a million students erupted in the biggest campus revolt in history. Over 450 colleges and universities and 150 high schools struck or closed their doors. Antiwar demonstrations were reported on 60 percent of the country's campuses.

Now Nixon resorted to covert, illegal, and unconstitutional methods to overcome dissent. In a hysterical response to swelling opposition, he approved a rich variety of "dirty tricks"—opening people's mail, tapping their phones, burglarizing their offices, placing spies in the peace movement, using police provocations. It fixed a pattern of criminal action by the executive that eventually brought Nixon's downfall and the collapse of his policy in Indochina.

When reports appeared of the poisonous effects of U.S. chemical warfare upon Vietnam's fields and streams, people concerned with the environment and ecology were won to the peace cause. A powerful push for peace came when Daniel Ellsberg leaked the "Pentagon Papers." What antiwar leaders had long asserted was now proved in these documents to be true. Here was the secret history of how the United States made its decisions about Vietnam. The official documents demonstrated that Vietnam was the planned outcome of aggressive U.S. policy in Southeast Asia. And they made clear how the U.S. leadership had, all along, deceived the American people into believing otherwise.

Just before the 1972 elections, Nixon negotiated peace terms with North Vietnam. But South Vietnam rejected the terms. Then Hanoi demanded some changes of its own. Nixon's answer was to order the most savage bombing raids in history against North Vietnam that Christmas week to force Hanoi to accept his demands. Again the antiwar movement went into the streets to protest. Finally, in January 1973, the long-sought peace agreement was concluded in Paris. Washington recognized "the independence, sovereignty, unity and territorial integrity" of Vietnam as set forth in the 1954 Geneva agreements.

But the peace movement knew the struggle was not really over. It determined to keep up the pressure beyond the war's apparent end. To bolster the peace settlement, the activists pressed Washington to respect the Paris accords and tried to stop the U.S. bombing of Cambodia and Laos. The war went on another two years, by proxy, with the United States conducting it through its puppet government in South Vietnam. Finally, when Nixon's regime crumbled during the Watergate crisis of 1973, Congress cut off funds for U.S. bombing of Cambodia. Despite heavy U.S. support, the war effort in South Vietnam and Cambodia collapsed. Then, in the spring of 1975, a major communist offensive shattered the remnants of the South Vietnamese military forces and unified the land under communist control.

The peace movement rejoiced in the ending of the long war. But few felt that the communist victory would mean freedom for a country that had known neither peace nor freedom for many generations.

What was lost in Vietnam? Not only a war. It

was confidence that the United States had the right answers to the problems of a troubled world. The foreign policy of the years since World War II had proved a failure. Washington's preference for violence, for military power to counter social and political change in smaller nations, had been shown not to work. Most activists for peace hoped that the United States would learn from the agony of Vietnam.

CHAPTER SEVENTEEN

To Murder the Future?

Daily, more than ten thousand people walk past the glossy black V-shaped marble wall in Washington on which are carved the names of 57,939 Americans who died in Vietnam. Many of these visitors—men, women, and children—step up to feel the cold texture of the engraved names of the dead. They must touch them, the names of their dead; it is not enough just to read them. Sometimes, even in soaking rain, they stand there long, staring at the name of a son, a father, a brother, a husband, a friend.

"Why were they killed?" a child asks.

Many answers have been offered. But one comes up repeatedly. Apparently a major purpose behind the war for all the Presidents from Kennedy to Nixon was to avoid the political embarrassment of withdrawal.

So trivial a goal for all those Americans—and several million Vietnamese, Laotians, and Cambodians—to die for.

Yet Vietnam is but one example of wars America entered for doubtful reasons and fought beyond hope of useful results. Like many of the other wars discussed in this book, it needs to be remembered.

To remember what happened will help us to avoid repeating disasters in new forms. There are signs that some do remember and did learn something. The myth that America never loses a war crumbled in Vietnam. The image of ourselves as a righteous nation was damaged. We are not always the "good guys." We found we are neither invincible in war nor infallible in moral judgment.

Early in the 1980s the United States became deeply involved in Central America. Wherever a popular revolution replaced a repressive regime, the alarm rang. Again the domino theory was sounded in Washington, stirring the same currents of dissent that troubled the country during the Vietnam War. Whenever alarms are raised about our national security being in danger, we might recall our war with Mexico, or our war with Spain—times when we were stampeded into military ventures.

There is much the United States could do to help make Latin America stable, to encourage democracy and build prosperity. To use threats and armed force instead of diplomacy and peaceful negotiation is to turn minor problems into colossal defeats.

That is even more true in the confrontation between the two superpowers. Today the world confronts the imminent possibility of a nuclear holocaust. An absolutely evil, human-made catastrophe, beyond any experience in history. With a power rising out of the development of scientific knowledge and its technological use, man can destroy life itself and make the earth uninhabitable.

The two superpowers—the United States and the Soviet Union—now have more nuclear bombs on both sides than there are targets. Between them they possess more than fifty thousand nuclear warheads, packing the explosive force of 1 million Hiroshimas. With a level of blast, of fire, of radioactivity, of the loss of the ozone layers, a nuclear exchange would destroy all life itself except the insects and grass.

If a nuclear holocaust should occur, there will be no "outside" to flee to, or from which rescue might be managed. Survival is a wholly unrealistic expectation. The experts doubt whether a nuclear conflict could be controlled. Its beginning would therefore mean our ending—*the death of life itself, of the species itself.*

With that unbearable prospect in mind, does it matter much if you or anyone else decides to become a conscientious objector? Not in the sense that your personal refusal to fight will prevent the killing of others. For, before armies could be ordered into action, the signal could be given for nuclear missiles to wipe out hundreds of millions of human beings. But that truth about modern means of war only underscores the need for nonviolent resisters to muster all their strength, intelligence, and imagination to find practical ways to end the possibility of nuclear extinction.

On June 12, 1982, a million Americans assembled in New York's Central Park to call for nuclear disarmament. It was the greatest success of the American peace movement to that time. It signaled the rapid growth of peace groups that within two years would swell to over thirteen hundred organizations—national, regional, and local. Physicians, scientists, lawyers, teachers, businessmen, labor, artists, neighbors formed their own groups to work for a stable and enduring peace. They published leaflets and pamphlets and newspapers. They produced films and recordings. They sent out speakers, they urged antinuke positions on political candidates, they regis-

A million people demonstrated their support for nuclear disarmament at a rally in New York's Central Park on June 12, 1982. It was the largest antiwar protest ever seen in America.

tered voters, they did mailings, they raised funds, they marched, they picketed, they telephoned, they wore buttons and slapped on car stickers, they demonstrated, they petitioned, they protested, they did—and are doing—anything and everything the imagination can devise to help reverse the arms race here and around the world.

Most of these peace groups are new in the field.

They add their voices and their strength to the older peace movement. The traditional peace churches are still very much in action, their power enhanced now by the U.S. Catholic bishops' war and peace pastoral letter and the programs and study sessions organized around that message in churches around the nation and the world. Though these hundreds of groups may differ on tactics, all are united by their passionate desire to prevent nuclear war. They have absorbed the urgency and uniqueness of the nuclear peril—what Jonathan Schell in his book *The Fate of the Earth* calls "the murder of the future."

While the peace seekers recognize that we are in a *new* time with regard to weapons, the nations operate as though they are in the *old* time before nuclear force. For the old purposes of national security, governments threaten to fire nuclear missiles at each other. This produces the absolute absurdity. For the sake of the national interest, they will murder us all.

And yet the senseless spending on nuclear arms continues. The policy makers in Washington seek to increase the nuclear arsenal in the vain pursuit of *winning* a nuclear war with the Soviet Union. Their plans will only accelerate the already frightening arms spiral. It would make nuclear war all the more likely.

But it need not happen. If each of us accepts the responsibility for the earth's survival, we can make a difference. The power of an aroused and informed public is great; we saw its influence during Vietnam. A worldwide movement to avert a nuclear catastrophe is on the rise. In the United States, its immediate goal is to secure a verifiable freeze in the development, production, and deployment of nuclear arms by both America and the Soviet Union. The citizens' movement to control and reduce nuclear arms is engaged in a long and hard struggle. It musters the energy and intelligence of scores of national organizations and thousands of local groups who share the same objective.

Such grass-roots efforts win results. In 1983 such an effort secured the historic vote in favor of a nuclear freeze by a sizable majority of the U.S. House of Representatives. That same week the Roman Catholic bishops of the United States, by a margin of 238 to 9, ratified an unprecedented pastoral letter denouncing nuclear war. They called upon America's 51 million Catholics to help rid the world of nuclear weapons.

The newly reunited Presbyterian Church has called for a nuclear freeze. The Mennonites, Quakers, and other churches have taken the same stand. Earlier, in the fall of 1982, in the largest referendum

Picketing the White House is but one of the many and greatly varied ways peace groups use their strength and imagination to rouse America to the danger of nuclear extinction. By 1984 over 1300 organizations were working for a stable and enduring peace.

on any issue in U.S. history, millions of Americans approved freeze proposals in local elections across the country. They discovered that the nuclear arms race is as much a local issue as a national issue. It unleashed an enormous initiative and creativity in support of the movement for survival.

Most citizens are not questioning the country's need for a strong defense and the need to be ever vigilant of the Soviets. And they are not recommending unilateral or unverifiable arms reduction. They are saying that the arms race between the United States and the Soviet Union is leading the world to annihilation. And they insist that we act together to reverse that course.

The unpleasant truth cannot be avoided. Everyone knows there *is* a nuclear danger, and no escape from living with it. Most of us, if we could ban the bomb tomorrow, would do it. But political reality does not allow it. The superpowers have not yet come to any agreement that would reliably do away with nuclear weapons. This sad truth does not mean it won't happen in the future. It means we have to work harder at it, make a better and stronger effort.

Which is why the American Catholic bishops' pastoral letter says that nuclear deterrence is justifiable as the world stands now. Not as a purpose in itself, but as a step toward gradual disarmament. Deterrence is a means of preventing others from using nuclear weapons. The Russian arsenal deters the United States from pressing the button, and the U.S. arsenal has the same effect upon the Soviet Union.

The bishops agree that no country can "prevail" in a nuclear war. Victory and defeat are meaningless concepts in nuclear war: Everyone will perish as the earth is destroyed. Nor do the bishops believe in trying to achieve nuclear superiority. The nuclear arsenals both superpowers amassed as far back as twenty years ago were enough to inflict unacceptable damage. To develop and manufacture still more weapons means insane waste.

To support these principles, the bishops recommend a whole series of arms-control measures. They call for a general stop to the arms race, deep bilateral cuts in arsenals, a comprehensive test ban treaty, and removal of the short-range weapons, "which multiply dangers disproportionate to their deterrent value."

Arms-control agreements alone, the bishops caution, are not enough. They must go along with parallel efforts to reduce political tensions. The bishops say, "The fact of a Soviet threat . . . cannot be denied. . . . Americans need have no illusions about the Soviet system of repression" or about their nuclear buildup and deployment. Yet the bishops believe that the Soviet leaders can be deterred, and in more than one way. By negotiations, by awareness of our common humanity, and above all by the recognition "that everyone will lose in a nuclear exchange."

After all, is there any alternative to negotiation? Does anyone really believe that America can frighten the Soviet Union into submissiveness by an arms race? There is no way to peace but to get down to the hard work of talking. The two great powers must try to work from their common interest in survival.

Surely the American people have that concern in mind—survival. And happily for the pursuit of peace, a sizable part of the American public no longer stays silent when it sees its government make mistakes in foreign policy. They react to the danger of repeating past errors. They know American leaders can be guilty of intrigue, deception, secretiveness, lawlessness. They learned that dissent has its positive side and should never be crushed. It was only when dissent over Vietnam rolled high enough to reach into Congress and change many minds there that the policy of Presidents was obliged to change. We rediscovered the old belief that the truth will make us free. We must continue to say how we see things, and speak out for what we believe.

Bibliography

Titles marked with asterisks (*) are paperback editions. Those with daggers (†) are hardcover books also available in paperback.

Bacon, Margaret H. *The Quiet Rebels: The Story of the Quakers in America.* New York: Basic Books, 1969.

*Bainton, Roland H. *Christian Attitudes Toward War and Peace.* New York: Abingdon, 1960.

*Barnet, Richard J. *Roots of War.* New York: Penguin, 1972.

Baskir, Lawrence M., and Straus, William A. *Chance and Circumstance: The Draft, the War, and the Vietnam Generation.* New York: Knopf, 1978.

*Blainey, Geoffrey. *The Causes of War.* New York: Free Press, 1973.

*Brant, Irving. *The Bill of Rights.* New York: Bobbs-Merrill, 1965.

†Brock, Peter. *Pacifism in Europe to 1914.* Princeton: Princeton University Press, 1972.

_____. *Pacifism in the United States from Colonial Era to the First World War.* Princeton: Princeton University Press, 1968.

Chatfield, Charles. *For Peace and Justice: Pacifism in the United States, 1914–1941.* Knoxville: University of Tennessee Press, 1971.

Childress, James F. *Civil Disobedience and Political Obligation.* New Haven: Yale University Press, 1971.

†Cluster, Dick, ed. *They Should Have Served That Cup of Coffee.* Boston: South End Press, 1979.

*Cooney, Robert, and Michalowski, Helen, eds. *The Power of the People: Active Nonviolence in the United States.* Culver City, Calif.: Peace Press, 1977.

Curti, Merle E. *Peace or War: The American Struggle, 1636–1939.* New York: Norton, 1936.

*Day, Dorothy. *The Long Loneliness.* New York: Harper & Row, 1981.

De Benedetti, Charles. *The Peace Reform in American History.* Bloomington: Indiana University Press, 1980.

Draper, Theodore. "Falling Dominos," *New York Review,* October 27, 1983, pp. 6–19.

*Falk, Richard A., Kolko, Gabriel, and Lifton, Robert Jay, eds. *Crimes of War.* New York: Vintage, 1971.

Fine, Melinda, and Steven, Peter, eds. *American Peace Directory: 1984.* Cambridge, Mass.: Ballinger, 1984.

*Finn, James. *Protest: Pacifism and Politics.* New York: Random House, 1967.

Forest, James H. *Catholics and Conscientious Objection.* Rev. ed. New York: Catholic Peace Fellowship, 1981.

Gara, Larry. *War Resisters in Historical Perspective.* New York: War Resisters League, n.d.

*Gaylin, Willard. *In the Service of Their Country: War Resisters in Prison.* New York: Viking, 1970.

Giffin, Frederick C. *Six Who Protested: Radical Opposition to the First World War.* Port Washington, N.Y.: Kennikat Press, 1977.

Green, Martin. *Tolstoy and Gandhi, Men of Peace.* New York: Basic Books, 1983.

Gray, Harold S. *Character "Bad": The Story of a Conscientious Objector.* New York: Harper & Brothers, 1934.

*Hentoff, Nat. *Peace Agitator: The Story of A. J. Muste.* New York: Macmillan, 1963.

†Jantzen, Steven. *Hooray for Peace, Hurrah for War.* New York: Knopf, 1971.

Jones, Rufus M. *The Quaker in the American Colonies.* Reprint. New York: Russell & Russell, 1962.

Kennan, George F. "Zero Options," *New York Review,* May 12, 1983, p. 3.

†Kennedy, David M. *Over Here: The First World War and American Society.* New York: Oxford, 1980.

King, Martin Luther. *The Trumpet of Conscience.* New York: Harper & Row, 1967.

Lynd, Alice, ed. *We Won't Go: Personal Accounts of War Objectors.* Boston: Beacon Press, 1968.

*Maclear, Michael. *The Ten Thousand Day War: Vietnam 1945–1975.* New York: Avon, 1981.

Mayer, Peter, ed. *The Pacifist Conscience.* New York: Holt, Rinehart & Winston, 1966.

Miller, William Robert. *Nonviolence: A Christian Interpretation.* New York: Schocken Books, 1964.

*Muste, A. J. *Of Holy Disobedience.* Wallingford, Pa: Pendle Hill Publications, 1952.

Pacifica Studies on Conscientious Objection. Glendora, Calif.: Pacifica Library Associates, 1942.

Patterson, David S. *Toward a Warless World: The Travail of the American Peace Movement, 1857–1914.* Bloomington: Indiana University Press, 1976.

Peck, Jim. *We Who Would Not Kill.* New York: Lyle Stuart, 1958.

Peterson, H. C., and Fite, Gilbert C. *Opponents of War, 1917–18.* Madison: University of Wisconsin Press, 1957.

*Rivkin, Robert S., and Stichman, Barton F. *The Rights of Military Personnel.* New York: Avon, 1977.

Robinson, Jo Ann Ooiman. *Abraham Went Out: A Biography of A. J. Muste.* Philadelphia: Temple University Press, 1981.

*Schlissel, Lillian, ed. *Conscience in America: A Documentary History of Conscientious Objection in America, 1757–1967.* New York: Dutton, 1968.

*Seeley, Robert A. *Handbook for Conscientious Objectors.* Philadelphia: Central Committee for Conscientious Objectors, 1982.

*Sibley, Mulford Q., ed. *The Quiet Battle: Writings on the Theory and Practice of Nonviolent Resistance.* New York: Doubleday Anchor, 1963.

Surrey, David S. *Choice of Conscience: Vietnam Era Military and Draft Resisters in Canada.* New York: Praeger, 1982.

*Thompson, E. P., and Smith, Dan, eds. *Protest and Survive.* New York: Monthly Review Press, 1981.

†Walzer, Michael. *Just and Unjust Wars: A Moral Argument with Historical Illustrations.* New York: Basic Books, 1977.

†_____. *Obligations: Essays on Disobedience, War and Citizenship.* Cambridge, Mass.: Harvard University Press, 1970.

*Wells, Ronald A., ed. *The Wars of America: Christian Views.* Grand Rapids: Eerdmans, 1981.

Wieseltier, Leon. "The Great Nuclear Debate," *The New Republic* January 10 and 17, 1983, pp. 7–37.

Wittner, Lawrence S. *Rebels Against War: The American Peace Movement, 1941–1960.* New York: Columbia University Press, 1969.

Words of Conscience. Washington, D.C.: National Interreligious Service Board for Conscientious Objectors, 1980.

Wright, Edward Needles. *Conscientious Objectors in the Civil War.* Philadelphia: University of Pennsylvania Press, 1931.

Zahn, Gordon C. *War, Conscience and Dissent.* New York: Hawthorn, 1967.

Zampaglioni, Gerardo. *The Idea of Peace in Antiquity.* Notre Dame, Ind.: University of Notre Dame Press, 1973.

Note: By far the most exhaustive reading list on the many aspects of nonviolence and the peace movement can be found in Cooney and Michalowski's *The Power of the People*. It also includes a list of nonviolent organizations in America, arranged by state. Another excellent list is supplied in Seeley's *Handbook for Conscientious Objectors*. It includes antiwar films and literary works. Fine and Steven's *American Peace Directory: 1984* lists vital information on over 1,350 peace-oriented groups. These books are cited above.

Index

Numbers that appear in *italics* refer to pictures.

275

Neutrality Act, 186
New England Non-Resistant
    Society, 77, 91
New York Peace Society, 70
Nicaragua, 180
Niebuhr, Reinhold, 182
Nixon, Richard M., 228, 254–56,
    258
"No More War" parades, 177, *178*
Nobel laureates' peace call, 222
Nobel Peace Prize, 146, 225
Non-Conscription League, 155
nonviolent resistance, 13, 19–20,
    188, *197*, 205–7, 214, 217, 225;
    use by King, 223–25; against
    Nazi occupation of Norway,
    189–90. *See also* civil dis-
    obedience, draft resistance,
    pacifists, war resistance, etc.
Norris George W., 149
nuclear arms race, 213
nuclear freeze, 264
nuclear test ban treaty, 227. *See
    also* disarmament.
nuclear war danger, 6, 171,
    212–13, 260–68

O'Hare, Kate Richards, 157
Oneida Community, 117
Origen, 14–15
Oxford Pledge, 177

pacifists: as absolutists, 11, 50,
    81, 94, 110, 117, 160–61, 188; in
    American Revolutionary War,
    40–54; conflicts over force to
    overthrow slavery, 102–3; in
    Crusades, 20; dilemma over
    fighting Hitler, 188; division
    over imperialism, 136–37; in

early Christian era, 13–16;
    Garrison's view of, 78; and
    Hebrew prophets, 13; as
    instrument of reform, 147; in
    invasion threat, 189; and
    national liberation wars,
    100–101; opposition to fascism,
    184; opposition to militarism in
    schools, 125; promotion of
    disarmament, 179; in the
    Reformation, 22–23; selective,
    12, 163–64; Tolstoy's influence
    on, 128–30; and Vietnam War,
    237; weak in World War II,
    204. *See also* conscientious
    objection, Mennonites,
    nonviolent resistance,
    Quakers, women, etc.
Paine, Thomas, 45
Parker, Theodore, 87
Patton, George S., 212
Peace Association of Friends in
    North America, 126
peace churches, 21–23, 40–44, 80,
    110, 161, 219, 263. *See also
    specific religions.*
peace congresses, 125, 126, 139
peace fairs, 96
peace movements: actions urged
    by, 71, 123, 175, 218; elites'
    role in, 138–41; groups formed,
    70, 72, 74, 77, 92, 123, 126,
    138, 175–80, 217, 225, 226,
    236; methods used by, 82, 93,
    95, 124, 176, 218, 261–62, *262,
    265*; of radical pacifists, 217–18;
    studies of cause and cure of
    war, 140, 176
peace pamphlets for children, 126
peace pledges, 95–96, 147, 177

279